BARRON'S

EMILY BRONTË'S

Wuthering Heights

BY

Frances McCarthy

SERIES EDITOR

Michael Spring
Editor, *Literary Cavalcade*
Scholastic Inc.

D0366146

BARRON'S

BARRON'S EDUCATIONAL SERIES, INC.
Woodbury, New York / London / Toronto / Sydney

ACKNOWLEDGMENTS

We would like to acknowledge the many painstaking hours of work Holly Hughes and Thomas F. Hirsch have devoted to making the *Book Notes* series a success.

All inquiries should be addressed to:
Barron's Educational Series, Inc.
113 Crossways Park Drive
Woodbury, New York 11797

Library of Congress Catalog Card No. 84-18426

International Standard Book No. 0-8120-3448-1

Library of Congress Cataloging in Publication Data
McCarthy, Frances.
   Emily Brontë's Wuthering Heights.

   (Barron's book notes)
   Bibliography: p. 78
   Summary: A guide to reading "Wuthering Heights" with
a critical and appreciative mind encouraging analysis
of plot, style, form, and structure. Also includes
background on the author's life and times, sample tests,
term paper suggestions, and a reading list.
   1. Brontë, Emily, 1818–1848. Wuthering Heights.
[1. Brontë, Emily, 1818–1848. Wuthering Heights.
2. English literature—History and criticism] I. Title.
II. Series.
PR4172.W73M38 1984   823'.8   84-18426
ISBN-0-8120-3448-1 (pbk.)

PRINTED IN THE UNITED STATES OF AMERICA

456   550   987654321

CONTENTS

ADVISORY BOARD

HOW TO USE THIS BOOK

You have to know how to approach literature in order to get the most out of it. This *Barron's Book Notes* volume follows a plan based on methods used by some of the best students to read a work of literature.

Begin with the guide's section on the author's life and times. As you read, try to form a clear picture of the author's personality, circumstances, and motives for writing the work. This background usually will make it easier for you to hear the author's tone of voice, and follow where the author is heading.

Then go over the rest of the introductory material—such sections as those on the plot, characters, setting, themes, and style of the work. Underline, or write down in your notebook, particular things to watch for, such as contrasts between characters and repeated literary devices. At this point, you may want to develop a system of symbols to use in marking your text as you read. (Of course, you should only mark up a book you own, not one that belongs to another person or a school.) Perhaps you will want to use a different letter for each character's name, a different number for each major theme of the book, a different color for each important symbol or literary device. Be prepared to mark up the pages of your book as you read. Put your marks in the margins so you can find them again easily.

Now comes the moment you've been waiting for—the time to start reading the work of literature. You may want to put aside your *Barron's Book Notes* volume until you've read the work all the way through. Or you may want to alternate, reading the *Book Notes* analysis of each section as soon as you have finished reading the corresponding part of the original. Before you move on, reread crucial passages you don't fully understand. (Don't take this guide's analysis for granted—make up your own mind as to what the work means.)

Once you've finished the whole work of literature, you may want to review it right away, so you can firm up your ideas about what it means. You may want to leaf through the book concentrating on passages you marked in reference to one character or one theme. This is also a good time to reread the *Book Notes* introductory material, which pulls together insights on specific topics.

When it comes time to prepare for a test or to write a paper, you'll already have formed ideas about the work. You'll be able to go back through it, refreshing your memory as to the author's exact words and perspective, so that you can support your opinions with evidence drawn straight from the work. Patterns will emerge, and ideas will fall into place; your essay question or term paper will almost write itself. Give yourself a dry run with one of the sample tests in the guide. These tests present both multiple-choice and essay questions. An accompanying section gives answers to the multiple-choice questions as well as suggestions for writing the essays. If you have to select a term paper topic, you may choose one from the list of suggestions in this book. This guide also provides you with a reading list, to help you when you start research for a term paper, and a selection of provocative comments by critics, to spark your thinking before you write.

THE AUTHOR AND HER TIMES

A graveyard nearly encircled the Haworth parsonage, where Emily Brontë lived for most of her thirty years. Emily's mother died in that parsonage in 1821, when the girl was three. Two years later, Emily and her three older sisters were sent to boarding school, where two of them, Maria and Elizabeth, succumbed to typhus and died. Other than such bare, depressing facts as these, we know very little about Emily Brontë's life.

Jumping from the life of any writer into his or her work is risky, but usually there is something to narrow the gap just a bit: letters, diaries, or confidences to friends. There is almost nothing like that of Emily's, so you have few clues as to how she felt about any of these facts. In part this is because Haworth is in Yorkshire, in northern England, far from the cultural circles of London. But even by the standards of a quiet country town, Emily was reclusive. The other surviving children—Charlotte, Branwell, and Anne—at least talked to other people. And since *Wuthering Heights* was not widely read or appreciated in its day (in fact, it was not generally recognized as a masterpiece until this century), no one bothered to find out anything about its author. The person who was pressed for information was Charlotte, after the success of her second novel, *Jane Eyre*. In the strong light shed on her, you catch glimpses of her more gifted younger sister.

The Brontë children were left largely to their own devices. Their father Patrick, the vicar, was eccentric and domineering. He spent most of his time in his study and even took his meals there. The children's aunt, who moved to the parsonage shortly after their mother's death, didn't like the cold, bleak, isolated town of Haworth, and stayed mostly in her room with the fire banked high and the door firmly shut. Discipline was lax; circumstances seemed to foster an independence of spirit.

The practical Charlotte and the submissive Anne went to school and found jobs as governesses; but Emily rarely left home, and little is known of what she did at Haworth. She wandered over her beloved moors, did the ironing, baked the bread, listened to the servants' stories.

How could such an inexperienced young woman as Emily Brontë have written so convincingly in *Wuthering Heights* of passionate love? As far as is known, Emily showed no romantic interest in anyone, but there were plenty of examples of the frustrations of love around her. (And surely she got some inspiration from books she read.) A young curate was attentive and flattering to all the sisters and to a friend Charlotte made at school; Anne was the only one who took him seriously, and her heart was broken. Charlotte agonized over an unrequited passion for the married head of the school in Brussels. And then there was Branwell.

A brilliant conversationalist, Branwell started hanging around bars in his teens, and if a stranger stopped by, he would entertain him for the price of a night's drinks. At first all the family's hopes were pinned on him, but it soon became clear that he wouldn't even be able to hold down a job on his own. Anne eventually got him a position as tutor for the Robinson family of Thorp Hall, where she was governess, and he fell wildly in love with the mistress of the place. Either because the husband found out, or because the wife tired of him, he was dismissed, and spent the rest of his short life addicted to alcohol and opium.

While Branwell was devoting himself to his love affair, his three sisters were busy writing. Charlotte had found some of Emily's earlier poems, and persuaded Emily to contribute to a book of verse by all three sisters, to be financed by money left them by their aunt. The three picked the pseudonyms of Currer [Charlotte], Ellis [Emily], and Acton [Anne] Bell, and their literary careers began. Turning from poetry to fiction, Charlotte wrote *The Professor* and *Jane Eyre;* Emily, *Wuthering Heights;* and Anne, *Agnes Grey*—all under their pseudonyms. Charlotte and Anne soon revealed their true identities; while Emily, true to form, forbade her sisters to reveal anything about her.

Two months after the "Bells" were unmasked, in September 1848, Branwell died. His dissipation had been to much for the frail Brontë constitution to bear. Emily herself caught cold the day of the funeral, the last day she ever went outdoors. Consumption took hold quickly. She wasted away before her anguished sisters but continued to see to her chores, refusing medical attention. On December 19, at the age of thirty, she died, unaware that her only novel would some day be recognized as a masterpiece.

Anne died half a year later, at the age of twenty-nine. Charlotte died at the age of thirty-eight. Patrick Brontë lasted another six years; he had outlived all his children.

THE NOVEL

The Plot

Mr. Lockwood, the narrator, has just rented a large, secluded house called Thrushcross Grange in the desolate moors of Yorkshire in northern England. When he goes to visit his landlord, a Mr. Heathcliff, who lives a few miles away at a smaller place called Wuthering Heights, he finds his new neighbor surly and quarrelsome. Forced to spend the night there because of a snowstorm, he dreams of a ghost calling itself Catherine Linton. Back at the Grange, he asks his housekeeper, Ellen (Nelly) Dean, to tell him about the strange household at Wuthering Heights.

Mrs. Dean's story begins thirty years before, when Wuthering Heights was the home of a respectable family called the Earnshaws. After a visit to Liverpool, Mr. Earnshaw has brought home a stray gypsy lad, whom he calls Heathcliff, to raise with his own children, Hindley and Catherine. Catherine feels a special closeness with Heathcliff, but Hindley hates him because the gypsy boy is Mr. Earnshaw's favorite. Shortly after his father dies, Hindley comes home from school with a new wife, and forces Heathcliff into the role of servant. Cathy takes Heathcliff's side, and the two run wild together on the moors, eventually falling in love. On one of their rambles they are caught peeking into the windows of Thrushcross Grange, where the Lintons live. The Linton children, Edgar and Isabella, are afraid of the rough Heathcliff, but become fond of Catherine, who is forced to stay with them for several weeks to recover from the bite of their watchdog.

When Cathy returns home, she's dressed like a lady and has given up her wild ways. She laughs at Heathcliff's black, cross look, and he runs off in anger. Hindley's wife dies soon after bearing a son, and in his grief Hindley treats Heathcliff worse than ever. Cathy and Heathcliff have also been arguing intensely.

Thus when Edgar Linton proposes, Cathy accepts. Afterward she tells Ellen, the housekeeper, that Edgar is handsome and cheerful, and that he's going to be rich one day. It would degrade her to marry Heathcliff now, she says, even though she believes she belongs with him.

Unbeknownst to Cathy, Heathcliff has been listening, and when he hears her say it would degrade her to marry him, he runs away. Cathy is beside herself when she learns he's gone, and falls ill.

Three years later, Cathy and Edgar marry, and together with Ellen, whom they persuade to come with them, make their home at Thrushcross Grange. The young couple have been happy together for six months when Heathcliff returns, a rich and educated man. He stays at Wuthering Heights with his old enemy Hindley, who's now a drunk. When Heathcliff visits Thrushcross Grange, Cathy is delighted to see him. Isabella Linton soon falls in love with the transformed Heathcliff. Cathy and Edgar, are both enraged, but for different reasons. Although Heathcliff thinks that Isabella is silly and weak, he pursues her in order to get revenge on Edgar and, perhaps, to get her property. Shortly after, Cathy falls ill. Delirious with fever, she imagines herself back with the young Heathcliff. While she lies ill, he and Isabella elope.

By the time the newlyweds return to live at Wuthering Heights, Cathy is sufficiently recovered to recognize Heathcliff when he sneaks into her room one day. Each accuses the other of betraying their love. That night Cathy dies in premature childbirth. When Heathcliff learns of her death, he beats his head against a tree and begs her ghost to haunt him.

Meanwhile, Isabella's love for Heathcliff has turned to hate. The day after Cathy's funeral, Isabella flees to Thrushcross Grange to confide her troubles in Ellen. Hindley, driven mad by the knowledge that he gambled away his property to Heathcliff, had tried to kill him the night before. In the ensuing struggle, Heathcliff had seriously injured Hindley. Isabella escapes to the south of England, and six months later Hindley dies.

Twelve years pass. Hareton, Hindley's son, grows up at Wuthering Heights with Heathcliff, who raises him to be proud of his ignorance and bad temper. Cathy and Edgar's daughter, also named Catherine, grows up at Thrushcross Grange, where Edgar gives her the love he once lavished on his wife. Cathy's told nothing about Wuthering Heights or Heathcliff.

Edgar hears that his sister Isabella is dying, and goes south to see her and the son, Linton, she bore not long after leaving Heathcliff. Edgar brings Linton home to Thrushcross Grange after Isabella dies, but the next day Heathcliff claims his son. Cathy doesn't see Linton again until three years later, when she meets Heathcliff for the first time.

Heathcliff takes Cathy to Wuthering Heights, where she is briefly reunited with Linton. Heathcliff tells Ellen that he intends the two to marry. Despite Edgar's ban on communication between the two households, Cathy secretly exchanges love letters with Linton until Ellen finds out and puts a stop to it. The next time Cathy runs into Heathcliff, he tells her that Linton is dying of love for her, but when she goes to see him, they fight. Heathcliff has turned Linton's natural peevishness into maliciousness. Cathy continues secretly to see the boy, however.

Edgar is dying, and fears for Cathy's future. Since he has no male heir, the property will pass to Linton, his sister's son. The only way Cathy can stay at Thrushcross Grange is to marry Linton. Shortly after Edgar dies, Linton also succumbs, and Heathcliff claims Thrushcross Grange in his late wife's name.

The major portion of Ellen Dean's story ends here. Lockwood leaves Yorkshire for a while. A year passes. Then Lockwood returns, and Ellen tells him what has happened in the interim. When Hareton, Hindley's son, and Cathy fell in love, a strange change came over Heathcliff. He lost interest in his revenge, yearning only to be again with his Cathy, and finally died.

As the story ends, Hareton and the younger Cathy are to be married.

The Characters

The characters in *Wuthering Heights* are sometimes compared to figures in myths, ballads, fairy tales, or dreams because they are rarely seen engaged in the more social commonplaces of everyday life. Edgar Linton, for instance, is said to be fun to talk to,

Genealogical Table

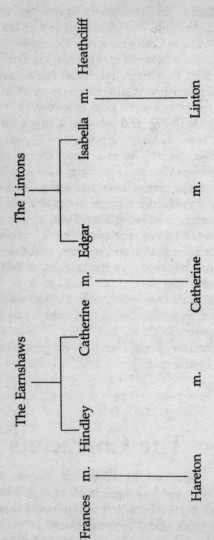

but you are given no idea what he talks about. Nor are you shown how characters act when they are outside the tight knot of Wuthering Heights and Thrushcross Grange, the two households that dominate the novel. Each character is generally of one of two types—the Wuthering Heights type (strong, passionate, stormy) or the Thrushcross Grange type (passive, civilized, calm). The obvious contrast is between Heathcliff and Edgar.

Heathcliff

Charlotte Brontë, in defending her sister's book to the readers of her day, never defended the character of Heathcliff. "He stands unredeemed," she wrote in her preface to the novel, "never once swerving in his arrow-straight course to perdition." She went on to question whether it was even right or advisable to create such beings.

Although modern readers, on the whole, are more sympathetic to Heathcliff, it's easy to understand Charlotte Brontë's position. To recite a catalogue of his sins is almost to retell the novel. You sympathize with him at first, when Hindley mistreats him and he loses Cathy, but when he returns transformed, and his plan of vengeance begins to unfold, your feelings change. You begin to question his love for Cathy. Was it selfish, not true love at all, but an obsession? Can love exist so intertwined with jealousy, hatred, and anger?

Mrs. Dean says that Heathcliff is greedy, and Cathy herself tells him he's close and covetous. His name is generally surrounded with words like *hell*, *devil*, *diabolical*, *infernal*, and *fiendish*. Worst of all, he's unrepentant. "I've done no injustice," he says at the end of the book.

The author's contemporaries were upset that such an evil character loomed so large in her book. In looking to identify the source of that sense of evil, some modern readers claim that Heathcliff represents a specifically sexual energy that Emily Brontë, a true Victorian, was bound to denounce.

Simply to condemn Heathcliff, however, is to ignore the real sympathy for him, even identification with him, that Emily Brontë evokes from her readers. People have seen Heathcliff in two very different lights:

1. *As a rebel.* Heathcliff, a friendless laborer, is mistreated by the landed gentry. He loses his true love to a man with wealth and a higher social position. He takes revenge by seizing control of Thrushcross Grange and Wuthering Heights. In this view, his revenge is an assertion of his dignity as a human being, and right is on his side.

2. *As a person committed to a higher love.* That is, a person committed to a love beyond the conventional notions of religion or morality. When Heathcliff identifies himself with Cathy ("I cannot live without my life! I cannot live without my soul!"), this is not selfishness; he is describing a love that holds nothing back. And he remains true to his love even when Cathy has betrayed him for Edgar. When he returns from his three-year exile, he plans at first to have revenge only on Hindley and to "look in" at Thrushcross Grange and make sure Cathy is happy. But his suffering overwhelms him, and he starts to torment others, especially Isabella, Edgar Linton's sister.

His revenge is thus a horrible deflection of his love for Cathy, and his greatest crime—and the source of all his later ones—is not to forgive her on her deathbed. It is only when he finds himself reconciled to her spirit that he abandons his cruelty toward Hareton and the younger Cathy.

Catherine Earnshaw, later Mrs. Edgar Linton

There are, in a sense, two Catherines: the one who roams wildly over the moors with Heathcliff, who races him barefoot when she loses her shoes in a bog; and the one who returns from Thrushcross Grange a lady, afraid that the dogs, and Heathcliff too, might soil her grand new dress. There is Heathcliff's Catherine, and there is Edgar's Catherine. They are not mutually exclusive, of course; even the wild Catherine is educated (unlike the young Heathcliff), and even the dressed-up Catherine is saucy and indulgent (unlike Edgar Linton).

You can see Catherine as either untrue to her own untamed nature, through pride or ignorance, or genuinely torn between two ways of being.

She herself admits that Heathcliff is "more herself" than she is, and that Edgar is as different from her "as a moonbeam from lightning, or frost from fire." Catherine's acceptance of Edgar's proposal, then, is a betrayal of Heathcliff and of herself. Why does she do it? Ellen says she's proud, and perhaps Cathy does want to be a great lady. Or perhaps Cathy's true desire is to free Heathcliff from Hindley's clutches. If so, her plan is foolish; neither Heathcliff nor Edgar would have gone along with it.

On the other hand, there is much evidence that Cathy is truly in conflict. She tells Ellen that Heathcliff's return has reconciled her to God and humanity; yet she describes him to Isabella as a "pitiless, wolfish man." When she tells Ellen of Edgar's proposal, she wonders whether Heathcliff even knows what being in love is, and despite the unconscious cruelty of the question, you wonder, too. His love seems so much larger, so much wilder, than human love.

If Cathy married Edgar for reasons other than love—ambition, or a desire to help Heathcliff—why doesn't she declare her love for Heathcliff on her deathbed? In that scene her passion is obvious, but it's as complicated as ever.

In a more conventional novel Catherine would be the heroine. Though her death comes before the midpoint of the story, her capacity for love is so great that her spirit—if not her actual ghost—haunts the rest of the novel.

Hindley Earnshaw

Readers who defend Heathcliff usually point to his mistreatment at Hindley's hands. You might think then that Hindley is the villain. However, nothing in this novel is that simple. Hindley is evil, cruel, dissolute; you can't deny or excuse his cruelty. But Hindley is also a victim—deprived of his father's love by the usurper Heathcliff, deprived of his beloved wife when she dies, and, finally deprived of Wuthering Heights itself by his enemy Heathcliff.

There is no doubt that Hindley is weak-willed. He is no match for Heathcliff, when quarreling over a horse as a boy or when gambling into the night as a man. He does not have the strengths usually associated with the other members of the Wuthering Heights household.

Edgar Linton

You first see Edgar through Heathcliff's eyes, as he peeks through the window at Thrushcross Grange. Edgar is weeping after a fight with Isabella over a little dog neither has any real interest in. Ellen also initially describes him as a coward and a weakling.

It's Cathy who responds to him from the beginning because he's pleasant, polite, refined, and educated (all Thrushcross Grange qualities). Later, after going to work for him, Ellen has nothing but praise for his kindness.

Edgar obviously loves Cathy, even though he doesn't always understand her, and their married life seems pleasant until Heathcliff returns. Edgar is also a good father—just compare him in this role to Hindley or Heathcliff.

And he is not quite the coward of Ellen's original description. When he orders Heathcliff out of his house, and Heathcliff responds angrily, Edgar strikes the bigger, stronger man.

Edgar, then, is the "angel" opposed to the "devil" Heathcliff. That, at least, is one way to see him. But have you ever known anyone who was *too* good? Such a person might be wonderful to be with— always charming and interesting, with good looks and money. Still, he or she may lack the ability to understand one's own struggles and fears.

Edgar at times does seem to lack this crucial understanding. Heathcliff speaks scornfully of leaving an ill Cathy to Edgar's "duty" and "humanity." You get the impression that Edgar isn't capable of the tumultuous passion that grips his rival.

Isabella Linton, later Mrs. Heathcliff

You don't see much of Isabella before she becomes infatuated with Heathcliff, and until then you assume she's much like her brother Edgar. When Ellen goes to live at Thrushcross Grange she compares Isabella and

Edgar to a honeysuckle bush embracing a thorn (Cathy). Ellen also says that Isabella is "a charming lady of eighteen; infantile in manners, though possessed of keen wit, keen feelings, and a keen temper, too, if irritated."

A shallow, weak creature, Isabella deceives herself into believing that Heathcliff loves her, and she marries him despite Edgar's warnings. After their marriage, when Heathcliff persecutes her, she exhibits behavior decidedly unlike the usual Thrushcross Grange qualities associated with Edgar; she rants and raves and speaks as fondly of revenge as does Heathcliff. Finally, when she can stand his abuse no longer, she leaves Heathcliff, displaying an unexpected strength of character, and goes off to a suburb near London to have her baby by herself.

Hareton Earnshaw

Hindley's son Hareton, the young Cathy, and Linton Heathcliff are often considered "echoes" of Heathcliff, the older Cathy, and Edgar Linton, respectively. Certainly Hareton has some Heathcliff-like qualities. He is rough, strong, foul-mouthed, brave, bad-tempered. Heathcliff himself compares his childhood to Hareton's and finds much in the boy to admire.

Hareton is a more moderate character than Heathcliff. He loves Heathcliff and defends him against Cathy's attacks. Hareton's love for the young Cathy, although strong, is not like Heathcliff's wild, all-consuming passion for her mother.

What are you to make of this moderation? You can see Hareton as a pale, diminished Heathcliff, a person who lacks Heathcliff's energy, craftiness, and commanding presence. Or you can see him as one of the few people in the novel who have learned to love. In the last scenes he and the young Cathy tease, not torment, each other. Perhaps it is the young lovers' example that helps Heathcliff finally discover some strange kind of peace in his own love.

Catherine Linton, later Mrs. Linton Heathcliff

Cathy can be seen, much like Hareton, as either a pale version of her mother or as another person who truly learns how to love.

Cathy is spirited, but is not as wild as her mother. She may wander over the moors, or go to the forbidden Wuthering Heights, but you don't see her carelessly losing her shoes in a bog. She may get angry, but she doesn't throw the temper tantrums of the older Cathy.

When Heathcliff arranges her marriage to Linton, he must take advantage of her tenderness to do so. This forces him to recognize that such soft feelings exist. Cathy may reject Hareton out of pride at first, but they are the ones finally able to escape the vicious circle of suffering in which the other characters were trapped.

Linton Heathcliff

Linton Heathcliff is sickly, spoiled, selfish, and sadistic. When young Cathy—the only person in years to show him any kindness—is locked up at Wuthering Heights by Heathcliff, her tears don't move him; they annoy him.

Linton can be seen as an "echo" of Edgar: he looks like him, his achievements are mental rather than physical, and he does get the girl. But to push this comparison too far is unfair to Edgar. Linton seems to possess the worst qualities of Edgar and Heathcliff.

Joseph

Joseph, the servant at Wuthering Heights, is a surly religious fanatic given to fits of highly articulate, if dialect-ridden, rage. (See "Glossary" for help in deciphering his speeches.) You can almost hear him bellow as you read. The question is, How seriously are you to take all his bluster? There is nothing amusing about the way Catherine presents him in her diary or the way Isabella describes his treatment of her, but Lockwood and Ellen's remarks about him are largely satirical. It may be that such a ridiculous figure is funny only at a distance.

The Narrators: Mr. Lockwood, Ellen (Nelly) Dean

Mr. Lockwood is the only real stranger to the moors. Presumably, he has had a life more like yours than like Heathcliff's or Cathy's. He's pleasant, courteous, and educated. Because of this, you can see him as a representative of ordinary, or conventional, judgment. Haven't you ever wanted to be free of everyone, as he does in the beginning of the book? And haven't you ever behaved as irrationally as he did when he rejected the young lady as soon as she returned his affections? So Lockwood's amazed horror at what happens when Heathcliff takes these natural impulses to their limits is your amazement and horror, too.

But there is another way to look at him. Since Emily Brontë is constantly undercutting him, you can see him as cold (his love problems, unlike Heathcliff's, stem from the young lady's *returning* his feelings), insincere (despite his declared love for solitude, he craves company and returns to Wuthering Heights when it's clear he's not wanted), and arrogant (he assumes that the younger Cathy doesn't fall in love with him because she can't recognize "a better class of people").

Your perspective on Lockwood is especially important when you read about his dream. He pulls the icy little hand of Cathy's ghost across a jagged windowpane until blood soaks the bedclothes. Certainly this is just as horrifying as anything Heathcliff does in the book. You can see Lockwood as an average person caught against his will in the violence of Wuthering Heights, or you can view him as no better than any of the other, wilder, characters in the story.

Ellen Dean's tempered, scolding tone is a counterpoint to the passionate ravings in the story she tells. She's sensible, pious without being fanatical, full of homespun wisdom, and admits her faults. She belongs to the moors; her position is never undercut the way Lockwood's is. Even Heathcliff respects her.

Ellen tries to be fair, and often acts as the "bridge" between the worlds of Thrushcross Grange and Wuthering Heights. She's the one who goes to see the newly married Heathcliffs; she's the one who takes Linton, and then the younger Cathy, to Wuthering Heights.

So why shouldn't you take her many opinions at face value? For one thing, she makes her bias obvious from the beginning, when she refers to the Lintons as "we." She is a Thrushcross Grange–type character, so you have to question her judgments of the Wuthering Heights passions. She is especially hard on the older Cathy, harder than most readers are.

Her actions often expose her limitations. Like Edgar, she tries to shelter others from the truth. She may not lie to Lockwood (and to you), but she lies to those caught up in the events of the story, especially to Edgar in the second half of the book. Her motives are good, but are her deceptions necessary or desirable?

She's also a bit of a tattletale. She tells Edgar that Heathcliff and Cathy are quarreling over Isabella, and she tells him that Cathy planned her fit. Both times the results are disastrous. Again, her motives are good—she wants to prevent greater violence later— but she only makes things worse. Can hers be a complete understanding of what's going on?

Other Elements

SETTING

There are only two houses in this novel: Wuthering Heights and Thrushcross Grange. The former is associated with the stormy side of life, the latter with the calm. Physically, there is a great contrast between these houses. Wuthering Heights is a strongly built and fierce-looking farmhouse. When Linton first sees it he is frightened by the "carved front and low-browed lattices, the straggling gooseberry bushes and crooked firs." The building is battered by severe winds during the frequent storms.

Thrushcross Grange, a large estate, is much more protected from the elements. It lies in a valley, and the park around it is enclosed by a stone wall. When Heathcliff first glimpses the drawing room through a window, he thinks it's heaven—all crimson, gold, and silver.

Yorkshire, where these houses are located, is a wild, bleak spot. There are few trees; slopes of black rock cut swathes through the heather, which is dull brown most of the year; little streams tumble everywhere. There's a lot of rain, a lot of mist, and a lot of snow. The people are taciturn, close fisted, and often brutal. There is no other world in the novel, and there was no other world for Emily Brontë.

THEMES

Wuthering Heights has always been controversial. Earlier generations argued over the quality of the novel. Readers today generally regard it as a high-quality work but argue over the meaning of its content. Some readers believe the novel's most significant theme is **revenge.** Until just before the end of the book, Heathcliff's revenge against those who have wronged him taints all the relationships at Wuthering Heights and Thrushcross Grange. Other readers see Heathcliff in a more favorable light and consider the most important theme to be **rebellion.** Heathcliff, a penniless outcase, eventually beats his oppressors at their own game. You can also widen your focus and say that the book mainly explores the **nature of love,** weighing definitions offered by Heathcliff and by Edgar. Their actions, and the feelings and actions of other characters, help you understand these definitions. You can also see *Wuthering Heights* as principally concerned with the **conflict between stormy and calm sides of life.** Wuthering Heights generally represents the stormy side, Thrushcross Grange the calm side. The conflict between these two ways of life causes great suffering until the marriage between Cathy and Hareton—a marriage in which both approaches to life are recognized and accepted.

STYLE

Emily Brontë's language is both spare and dense, which is why it's often compared to poetry. When you finish the novel, you have a firm sense of the bleak beauty of the moors, for instance, yet there are remarkably few descriptions of the landscape. What is there is immediately evocative.

Her prose is also unusually rhythmic, often violent and abrupt. The verbs themselves are almost hysterical, until the final paragraph, in which the moths "flutter" and the soft winds "breathe."

Her two sources of imagery are nature (animals, plants, fire, the land, the weather) and the supernatural (angel/devil, heaven/hell). These are evident in the words she uses and the mental pictures she evokes.

POINT OF VIEW

There is no single point of view in this novel. The story is told by Lockwood, by Catherine, by Ellen Dean, by Heathcliff, by Isabella, by the younger Cathy, and by Zillah, the other housekeeper. Since the author never explicitly tells you what to think, you must evaluate the story in the same way that you evaluate each of the characters telling it.

Lockwood and Ellen, who tell most of the story, appear more "normal" than most of the people they talk about (Lockwood is a conventional man about town, despite his brief sojourn to Yorkshire, and Ellen displays a practical, homespun wisdom), but you can't overlook their biases. Neither of them can appreciate the passion between Heathcliff and Catherine. You as a reader, can, however. You can see much more than any single character can tell you. Evaluating what each character says helps to draw you into the book.

FORM AND STRUCTURE

Part of what makes *Wuthering Heights* such an extraordinary novel is its complicated narrative structure. Although telling a story from different, limited points of view has become common in this century, when Emily Brontë was writing, most novels featured an omniscient narrator—someone (often, but not always the author) who was not a character in the book, but who could address the reader, comment on the action, and describe the thoughts and feelings of any of the people in the story. *Wuthering Heights* broke the mold; it is told solely by characters in the book, most notably Mr. Lockwood and Ellen Dean, although portions of Ellen's narrative include stories told to her by others.

The narrative itself consists of stories-within-stories-within-stories. Take a look, for instance, at Joseph's description of the dissipation at Wuthering Heights after Heathcliff's return. It is quoted *in* Ellen's warning to Isabella against Heathcliff, which is *in* her story to Lockwood, which is *in* Lockwood's story to you. Early readers were put off by this, seeing it as unnecessarily complicated and confusing; but most readers today view it as one of the novel's great strengths.

This book is full of doubles. There are two generations, each occupying half the chapters. There are two households, each with distinctive qualities. And the actions revolve around pairs of children (Heathcliff and Cathy, the younger Cathy and Linton, the younger Cathy and Hareton).

The Story

CHAPTER 1

It's through Lockwood's eyes that you first see Yorkshire, Heathcliff, and Wuthering Heights. He calls Yorkshire beautiful, but only because he finds the region removed and sparsely populated.

He calls Heathcliff a "capital fellow" and applauds him for his reserve. The unfriendlier Heathcliff is, the harder Lockwood pushes his way into his house, all the while declaring how much he sympathizes with Heathcliff's desire for solitude. Lockwood imagines that this desire springs from an aversion to emotional display (you'll soon see how wrong he is), and he hints that Heathcliff's story may be similar to his own. He himself fell in love with a young lady at the seaside, and as soon as she returned his affection, he lost interest.

NOTE: As you read Lockwood's narrative, bear in mind his odd personality and his often surprising (and inaccurate) interpretations of events and people's motives.

Wuthering Heights is strongly built—fortunately so, since "Wuthering" refers to the fierce winds that blow around the house. The name is symbolic, since the house is associated with the stormy side of life, as opposed to the calm of Thrushcross Grange. The servant Joseph is peevish, and dogs skulk in the recesses of the front room. The place looks as though it belongs to a farmer, but Heathcliff doesn't appear to be one. He is dark skinned like a gypsy and he has the dress and manners of a gentleman, or at least a country squire.

CHAPTER 2

Lockwood visits Wuthering Heights again, although he knows Heathcliff doesn't want him. A sinister tone creeps in. Heathcliff speaks so savagely to the young lady of the house that Lockwood accuses him of having a genuinely bad nature. Lockwood tries to figure out the relationships among his host, this woman named Mrs. Heathcliff, and another resident, a rudely dressed young man with a boorish manner but an air of haughtiness that seems out of place in a servant. The woman, he learns, is the widow of Heathcliff's late son. The young man's position remains unclear. He says merely that he is Hareton Earnshaw (you should recall, of course, that the inscription over the door described in the first chapter reads "1500 Hareton Earnshaw").

Lockwood realizes that a rising snowstorm will prevent him from finding his way home without help. Heathcliff refuses to guide him. He tells Lockwood that he can't sleep in the parlor, since he doesn't trust him. The young lady hints darkly of witchcraft. (Is she teasing? Everything seems possible in this house.)

This chapter ends, as the first one did, with a dog incident, but this one is much more frightening. Thinking that Lockwood has stolen a lantern, Joseph sets the dogs on him, and Heathcliff laughs as his guest bleeds. Lockwood is sick and dizzy afterward, and when he is forced to spend the night you get the first hint of the frustration that will play such a big part in this story.

CHAPTER 3

Zillah, the servant, leads Lockwood to a bedroom where, she says, Heathcliff never willingly lets anyone stay. She doesn't know why.

NOTE: Emily Brontë juxtaposes the mysterious with the mundane, throwing both into relief. Here it's a question of where Lockwood will sleep. Earlier, when he got such bizarre reactions when he asked who was related to whom, he was simply trying to have pleasant conversation over tea.

Before retiring, Lockwood notices a ledge on which "Catherine Earnshaw" is written in many different ways, interspersed with an occasional "Catherine Heathcliff" and "Catherine Linton." This is the first indication of the rift in Catherine's soul. (This also prefigures, in reverse, the history of the younger Cathy, whose last name changes from Linton to Heathcliff to Earnshaw.)

All the books, Lockwood notices, have a child's handwriting in the margins. Reading Catherine's words, he learns that now that her father is gone, Hindley—whom you haven't met yet—is treating Heathcliff atrociously. She describes a sad day when they rebelled against him and against Joseph's religious fanaticism. You may have identified with Lockwood up to now—however unwillingly—but Catherine is the first character really to engage your sympathies. Through Catherine, you get a different look at Heathcliff. No wonder he's so surly, after such an unpleasant upbringing.

Musing on the religious title of the book as well as on the notes in the margin, Lockwood falls asleep. He dreams that Joseph takes him to church to hear a sermon in which the preacher describes 490 sins, "odd transgressions that Lockwood never imagined before." In the dream Lockwood is horribly bored and finally calls on the parishioners to rise up and crush the preacher. At least for the present he is unconsciously siding with the rebellion described in the diary, and with Catherine.

But when he dreams again, this time of a ghost named Catherine Linton trying to get into the bedroom, Lockwood smashes the pane and draws her icy hand across the broken glass until the blood soaks the bedclothes. The violence of this is horrifying, especially since the ghost rouses your pity. However, you also sympathize with Lockwood's terror. When she persists, Lockwood cries out, and Heathcliff wakes him up. Lockwood screams that the house is haunted, describing the "fiend" he saw in his dream. Though Heathcliff yells back at him, Lockwood later overhears Heathcliff throwing open the window and sobbing for his dear Cathy to come in.

Notice how your picture of Heathcliff has changed. First he was "a capital fellow," then he had "a genuine bad nature," now you see him anguished, suffering.

NOTE: Is the ghost real?   Lockwood talks as if the ghost *were* real, even though he sees it in a dream. Heathcliff, too, in the second part of the book, believes in the reality of Cathy's ghost. Does Emily Brontë want you to believe in ghosts? Perhaps. But there are rational explanations for their appearances. Lockwood for instance, is in an overwrought state, and Heathcliff doesn't actually see the ghost until he's starved himself.

CHAPTER 4

This is the chapter in which Mrs. Dean begins her story. Lockwood has taken ill, and to pass the time he asks Mrs. Dean about his new neighbors. She compares Heathcliff's history to that of a "cuckoo." Cuckoo eggs are laid individually in the nests of other, smaller birds. When the eggs hatch, the young cuckoo, larger than its nestmates, displaces the natural offspring to become the sole focus of its foster parent's care.

This is remarkably similar to what happened at Wuthering Heights thirty years ago, when Mr. Earnshaw promised to bring his children presents from Liverpool, but instead brought back a dirty, ragged, gypsy lad.

As Mrs. Dean tells the story, they christened the boy Heathcliff, the name of a son who died at birth. Cathy soon takes to him, but Hindley plagues him. Hardened to such treatment, Heathcliff takes Hindley's abuse without complaint. By the time Earnshaw's wife dies, Heathcliff has wholly replaced Hindley in his father's affections.

When the two boys fight, Hindley calls Heathcliff "an interloper" and "an imp of satan," two epithets that will be used against him for the rest of the book. Heathcliff may be a usurper, but it's hard to blame him at this point since it's through no fault of his own.

A pattern is set: love can be capricious, and its consequences, devastating.

CHAPTER 5

Mr. Earnshaw rages so when he can't strike Hindley for being mean to Heathcliff that he sends his son away to a boarding school.

Cathy's faults, according to Ellen, arise from her high spirits. Ellen accuses her of loving Heathcliff too much—a judgment you may want to question. You have already heard Cathy's point of view in her diary, long before you had Ellen's, and Cathy was the first person with whom you really sympathized. You tend to put Ellen's criticisms of Cathy aside, and you will continue to do so even later, when Ellen's dislike becomes more pointed.

Cathy's sauciness also bothers her father, though his opinions may not count for much with you, given how unreasonable he is regarding his own son.

NOTE: In Mr. Earnshaw's last conversation with Cathy he asks her why she can't always be a good girl (she's quiet now because she's been sick). She replies, "Why cannot you always be a good man, Father?" Keep this in mind as you read, and ask yourself why these people behave so awfully to each other. Because of their suffering? Because of their evil natures? Because of the presence of a "demonic" Heathcliff? Is what the world calls "good" merely the result of sickness, as is the case here, or of a weak nature, as is the case with Edgar (which you'll see later in the novel)?

Mr. Earnshaw dies, with Cathy sitting beside him. She, Heathcliff, and Ellen cry out, broken. Joseph will have none of this grieving, for he pictures Mr. Earnshaw as a saint in heaven now. Later Ellen hears Heathcliff and Cathy comforting each other with beautiful images of heaven. It's the last time either will find comfort in anything conventional religion has to offer.

CHAPTER 6

Hindley comes home for his father's funeral with a wife, Frances, who delights in everything she sees except the preparations for the burial. Frances is afraid of dying.

NOTE: You know from movies the difference between the terms *surprise* and *suspense*. When a bomb goes off, you're surprised; when you know a bomb has been planted, but you don't know when it will explode, you're kept in suspense.

Ellen builds suspense by hinting at the future without letting you know for certain what will happen. She tells you, for instance, that she didn't know what Frances' shortness of breath and coughing meant. *You* know, however, and are left asking yourself, when will she die?

Emily Brontë gets you to turn the page by teasing you with glimpses into the future. You are always being given partial explanations, and you read on, hungry for the full story. Before you learn of Cathy and Heathcliff's early history, for example, you are given a quick look into Cathy's diary. And long before it happens, you know Mr. Earnshaw will die, and Hindley will become a tyrant.

When Frances expresses a dislike for Heathcliff, Hindley recalls his old hatred, and turns the boy into a laborer on the farm. Cathy teaches Heathcliff what she can as the two wander together over the moors.

One day Heathcliff returns alone after dark. Where is Cathy? Heathcliff explains to Ellen that he and Cathy peeked into the windows of Thrushcross Grange, and saw a beautiful room with crimson furniture, a pure white ceiling, and a silver and glass chandelier. It should have been heaven, but instead the Linton children—Edgar and Isabella—were fighting over a little dog. When the children heard a noise at the window, they cowered and cried for their parents.

NOTE: Now is a good time to compare the children, while there is still a "window" between them. Heathcliff and Cathy are wild, self-willed, strong, rebellious, and brave. Their passionate friendship excludes all others. Edgar and Isabella, who are safe inside a splendid house, are peevish, spoiled, and cowardly. At this point, choosing between the two sides is not hard. But as soon as Cathy is bitten by the Lintons' dog, and the Lintons welcome her and scorn Heathcliff, the distinctions begin to blur.

Because of the bite, which bleeds profusely, Cathy stays inside and Heathcliff returns alone to his place outside the window. Cathy, he sees, is very happy, "kindling a spark of spirit in the vacant eyes of the Lintons."

Because of this adventure, Hindley forbids Heathcliff to talk to Cathy, and his wife flatters Cathy into becoming a lady.

CHAPTER 7

When Cathy returns home after five weeks with the Lintons, she's dignified and well dressed. Heathcliff is still rough and dirty, and Cathy laughs at his black, cross expression. She apologizes and takes his hand, but looks with concern at her dress afterward to make sure it's still spotless. Ellen makes clear from her choice of details that she doesn't think much of Cathy's transformation.

After brooding for a day, Heathcliff tells Ellen he's going to be "good" (there's that word again—what does it mean to you?). Ellen helps him clean himself up, chatting happily.

Before Christmas dinner Edgar inadvertently insults Heathcliff, who responds by throwing a tureen of hot applesauce at him. The house is divided: Hindley beats Heathcliff, Ellen spitefully scrubs away at the victim's face, and Cathy lashes out at Hindley for speaking harshly to her old friend. During the carols Cathy sneaks off to where Heathcliff is locked up. Despite her new ladylike demeanor, all seems well between them, even better than before. The fact that their love has survived their separation makes it seem even more precious.

It's clear that Ellen, the voice of common sense, is still on Heathcliff's side. When Heathcliff announces that he'll have revenge on Hindley some day, Ellen doesn't make his plan sound evil. She understands him.

NOTE: Notice how Emily Brontë diverts your attention from the Heathcliff-Edgar conflict to the Heathcliff-Hindley conflict. This allows you to sympathize with Heathcliff without any slight to Edgar.

Mrs. Dean now tries to stop her narrative—it's getting late—but Lockwood presses her to continue.

CHAPTER 8

In this chapter you learn the meaning of thwarted love in the passionate world of Wuthering Heights. Soon after Hindley's son Hareton is born, his wife dies of consumption. Hindley takes to drink, cursing God and man alike. Tortured himself, he in turn treats Heathcliff in a way that would "make a fiend of a saint." (This "passing on" of suffering will be explored more fully in chapters 17 and 30.)

Catherine's conflicting feelings for Edgar and Heathcliff become increasingly apparent. She's cordial in the social world of Thrushcross Grange, but unruly in the dissipated atmosphere of Wuthering Heights. Ellen, whose dislike for her has become stronger, attributes Cathy's feeling for Edgar to ambition.

One afternoon when Hindley is gone from the house, Cathy quarrels with Heathcliff. She is still upset when Edgar arrives. In a fit of bad temper she pinches Ellen, slaps her then shakes baby Hareton, and strikes Edgar. When Edgar protests, Cathy tells him that she did not mean to be violent, and that she'll cry herself sick. Edgar thinks he should leave, but can't force himself to. Ellen can see that the passions unleashed that afternoon have made the two more open with each other—so open that they declare themselves in love.

Ellen has let you know many times that she doesn't like Cathy. Certainly, Cathy has behaved badly. Cathy admits that she can't hide or control her feelings, that her impulsiveness is part of her "Wuthering Heights" nature. But can you excuse her for her behavior, just because she can't control it?

NOTE: Hindley's dreadful mixing of love and cruelty at the beginning of the chapter is matched by Cathy's behavior later on. Love and cruelty—do the two emotions have anything in common? The two are so often related in *Wuthering Heights* that you have to wonder if they spring from the same source.

CHAPTER 9

Heathcliff saves Hareton's life when Hindley drunkenly drops him over the bannister. Heathcliff immediately regrets this missed opportunity for revenge; still, his instinctive reaction is good, and makes you wonder again why Cathy rejects him for Edgar. It doesn't seem to make sense, especially since Cathy is so articulate about her feelings:

> My love for Linton is like the foliage in the woods: time will change it, I'm well aware, as winter changes the trees. My love for Heathcliff resembles the eternal rocks beneath—a source of little visible delight, but necessary.

Ambition; a desire to help Heathcliff; a fear that Heathcliff may be beyond the accepted boundaries of love;—Cathy offers these reasons for accepting Edgar's proposal of marriage.

You can't help believing she is making a terrible mistake in accepting Edgar. She may need him, but she needs Heathcliff, too. Your suspicion that she and Heathcliff can never separate is confirmed by her reaction to Heathcliff's departure: she runs out into the night to find him, refuses to eat, lets the rain soak her through, and then stays up all night waiting for him. The next day, when Hindley says he's going to throw Heathcliff out of the house, Cathy swears she will go with him.

NOTE: Why does Heathcliff leave? In anger and humiliation? Is it to make himself worthy of her? To find the weapons for revenge? You can only speculate. In any case, even in his absence his relationship with Cathy manages to wreak havoc on Thrushcross Grange. Cathy gets sick from her walk through the rain in search of Heathcliff, and the older Lintons catch the fever and die.

Three years later Edgar and Cathy marry, which closes the first part of the book. The older generation is dead, and there is a resolution—however precarious—of the conflict between the two houses. The interloper is gone, and characters have regrouped themselves according to type: Edgar, Isabella and Ellen are at Thrushcross Grange; and Hindley, Hareton, and Joseph are at Wuthering Heights. Cathy is at Thrushcross Grange, but where her heart is, you will have to wait to see.

CHAPTER 10

Mrs. Dean broke off her narrative in the last chapter, and we're still in the present as this one begins. Lockwood has learned he'll be confined to bed until spring because of the fever. Despite his love of solitude, he misses people terribly.

Heathcliff visits, and surprises everyone with his friendly and entertaining behavior. What a difference between his present state and the savage "ploughboy" that ran off in the last chapter. His friendliness reinforces your sympathy for him. You're inclined to excuse his "genuine bad nature" the way Lockwood excuses him for causing his illness. When Lockwood asks Ellen Dean to continue her story, he refers to Heathcliff as the hero, and to Cathy as the heroine. You may see them in the same light, but your sympathies for them will soon be tested.

When Ellen Dean describes the Lintons' early married life, it's clear that she's firmly allied with Edgar, who preserves peace in the house by humoring Cathy. At first this doesn't seem to represent a change in Ellen's point of view, which has always been basically anti-Cathy, rather than pro-anyone else. But now that Heathcliff has returned, the Heathcliff-Edgar conflict will become more explicit, and she will—understandably—take Edgar's side.

When Ellen announces Heathcliff's return to the Lintons, she enters a scene of perfect domestic tranquility: from the window you can't even see Wuthering Heights, that place of storm. But as soon as the Lintons learn of Heathcliff's presence, Brontë's language again becomes violent. Cathy's embrace of Edgar *tightens to a squeeze*, and she *seizes* Linton's reluctant fingers, and *crushes* them into Heathcliff's.

When Ellen Dean first sees Heathcliff she doesn't recognize him—his looks, clothes, posture, and manners have greatly improved, at least in the eyes of the world. He puts Edgar to shame. You get the strange feeling that Heathcliff had made a pact with the devil. (How did he transform himself? You are never told.) He does seem not quite of this world anymore, and he shows a new harshness under his gentility. He says he struggled only for Cathy, and he warns her against trying to drive him away again.

In Chapter 9 you saw that Cathy wanted to have both Heathcliff and Edgar. She tries to perform the same balancing act here, too, and manages to keep them on an outwardly friendly footing for a while. The truce can't last for long, though, just as it couldn't that Christmas day years ago when Edgar ended up with applesauce on his face. This time the fight is caused by Isabella's infatuation for the new, gentlemanly Heathcliff.

NOTE: When Cathy tells Isabella to stay away from Heathcliff, she calls him "an arid wilderness of furze and whinstone"; that is, a wilderness with spiny shrubs and hard rock. He is not "a pearl-containing oyster," but a "wolfish" man who would crush Isabella like "a sparrow's egg."

Cathy's not the only character who uses plants and animals to describe the people in this book; everyone does. On almost every page someone is being compared to a tree, a honeysuckle, a dog, a lamb, or some other animal. Weather-related terms are used too (Edgar gets upset if a servant grows "cloudy" at one of Cathy's orders), and so is fire (Heathcliff's eyes are full of black fire). Since Emily Brontë lived in the country, it was only natural for her to find metaphors and symbols in the world that surrounded her. Nature and the supernatural (heaven-hell, angel-devil) are her frames of reference, the things by which all else is judged. This seems to place her closer temperamentally to Wuthering Heights than to Thrushcross Grange.

Cathy tells Heathcliff of Isabella's infatuation in the girl's presence (a surprising cruelty that will be amply punished), and Heathcliff is horrified. "You'd hear odd things if I lived alone with that mawkish, waxen face," he says; "the most ordinary would be painting on its white the colours of the rainbow, and turning the blue eyes black. . . ." It is a chilling statement that gives you a glimpse of the tortured man behind the gentlemanly veneer.

When Heathcliff asks about Isabella's property, Cathy says that Edgar will have many male heirs to wipe out his sister's claim. The question remains in your mind: is Cathy right to accuse him of greed? If not, why doesn't he deny Cathy's charges?

CHAPTER 11

Compare this opening with the opening of Chapter 9. In the earlier chapter Heathcliff saved baby Hareton from a dangerous fall. Ellen tells you that now Heathcliff has "saved" Hareton from acquiring an education and good manners, and has taught him to curse his father and go his own way. This is a good measure of the change in Heathcliff.

Keep Chapter 9 in mind as you read the rest of this chapter. In both, Cathy is asked to make an impossible choice between Heathcliff and Edgar, and ends up making herself sick.

When Ellen tells Cathy she saw Heathcliff embracing Isabella, Cathy is jealous. She confronts Heathcliff, who in turn accuses her of having treated him "infernally," expressing his anger even more strongly than he did at the first meeting. Yet when Edgar comes in and tells Heathcliff to leave, Cathy lashes out at her husband.

Here you have it at last, the showdown. It has been set up perfectly. The two rivals are now equals. Heathcliff is no longer a servant boy with all the "adults"—the elder Lintons, Hindley, and Joseph—against him. Each man is forced, to some extent, to fight on the other's terms. Heathcliff is at Thrushcross Grange, where Edgar has servants at his command. Edgar, the weaker of the two, is forced to fight physically, which is contrary to his nature.

NOTE: Most readers find that their sympathies are divided between these two rivals. Heathcliff, you feel, should have won Cathy, yet he is behaving abominably. The fight centers on a lock and key. Cathy has locked out the servants who are supposed to come to Edgar's aid, and when he tries to wrench the key from her, she throws it in the fire. For the rest of the book Heathcliff will often be the "keeper of the keys"—with all the freedom and the mastery over others that this implies. When he isn't, as he's not in this scene, he will break down the door. (This will be explored more fully in Chapter 27.)

There's no real resolution to the fight, of course. In trying to have both men, Cathy has ended up pleasing neither. When Heathcliff leaves, Edgar asks her to chose between them, and she refuses. Instead, she throws herself into a fit.

NOTE: Think now of the role Ellen plays in both scenes. Earlier she didn't tell Cathy that Heathcliff was listening, and then didn't inform her immediately of his departure. This time she's the one who tells Cathy of Heathcliff and Isabella's embrace, who tells Edgar that Heathcliff and Cathy are fighting, and who advises Edgar not to take Cathy's fit seriously. All of Ellen's intrigues have disastrous consequences; her meddling annoys everyone. In her defense you can argue that she was probably trying to avoid larger conflicts (Cathy and Heathcliff confronting each other in Chapter 9; Heathcliff insinuating himself further into Thrushcross Grange now). Whether events would have unfolded as they did without her interference is something you'll have to decide for yourself.

CHAPTER 12

Cathy shuts herself in her room and won't eat for two days. On the third day, Ellen enters the room and is shocked by the change. Cathy's face is wasted, and her manner is strange and exaggerated. Cathy's revenge on Edgar and Heathcliff is to kill herself. (Remember that when his wife died Hindley tormented others and started to drink himself to death. You will see more of this reaction.)

NOTE: Cathy says that Heathcliff set a trap over the nest of some lapwings; the older birds wouldn't come near it, so the babies died.

In a similar manner, many of the parent-child relationships in this book are distorted and cruel. Mr. Earnshaw detests Hindley; Hindley nearly kills Hareton; and Hindley as a substitute father mistreats Cathy and Heathcliff. Heathcliff, another substitute father, does everything he can to degrade Hareton. Often this is due to some outside agent, like the trap put over the lapwing nest. Heathcliff comes between Mr. Earnshaw and his son, and the death of Hindley's wife makes him lose any real interest in *his* son. In every case, it's the child who is vulnerable, almost as vulnerable as the baby lapwings.

Though Brontë's characters have painful childhoods, they also remember their youths as times of freedom and innocent, animallike joy. Soon after she speaks of the lapwings, Cathy says, "I wish I were a girl again, half savage and hardy, and free . . . and laughing at injuries, not maddening under them!"

You have contrasted the qualities of Wuthering Heights and Thrushcross Grange (stormy-calm, etc.). You should now add another: between child and

adult. The Wuthering Heights type characters—
Heathcliff and Cathy, especially—behave in many
ways like children even when they're grown up; they
have little self-control, for instance. The Thrushcross
Grange qualities of courtesy and self-restraint belong
more to the adult world. Does that explain why the
Thrushcross Grange characters, like Edgar and
Isabella, are the good parents? Emily Brontë's obvious
love for the vulnerable age of childhood softens you
toward many of the sins of those who live at Wuthering Heights.

It is Cathy's reliving of her childhood now that
makes you forget how difficult a person she was in
the previous chapter. She talks distractedly for a
while, and when she refers to a clothes press that is
not there, you know she's hallucinating. The clothes
press, you may remember from Lockwood's description in Chapter 3, is back in her old room at Wuthering Heights.

Cathy sees a face in the press (which is in fact a
mirror), and screams that the room is haunted. The
ghostly face she sees is, of course, her own. What a
chilling reminder of the "ghost" that Lockwood sees.
Cathy, imagining herself back home, relives her first
separation from Heathcliff (this is the scene that Lockwood reads in her diary). Longing to be out in the
heather, she throws open the window, just as she
tried to get *in* through the window in Lockwood's
dream.

In her delirium Cathy accuses Ellen several times of
being a witch, trying to harm her. Considering the
harm that Ellen has caused her, there may be a grain
of truth in this.

When Edgar comes in, he's horrified. He asks Cathy again if she loves Heathcliff, and again she hushes him. Why? Cathy's images of unhappiness in this scene have all revolved around her separation from Heathcliff.

As Ellen goes to get help, she notices Isabella's pet spaniel hanged with a handkerchief, and hears hooves galloping away. Emily Brontë tantalizes you by slowly giving you clues to the other drama of the night: the elopement of Heathcliff and Isabella.

CHAPTER 13

Cathy survives her fever, but she's convinced she's going to die soon anyway. In a lesser novel, the idea of a heroine dying of a broken heart would seem sentimental or hysterical. But here it's completely convincing.

NOTE: There are ghosts, which may or may not be real. There are premonitions of the deaths of Cathy, Mrs. Earnshaw, and Hindley's wife. Characters speak of being in heaven or hell in the same tone of voice you would use to speak of a visit across town. In *Wuthering Heights* the distinctions between life and death, and between the commonplace and the extraordinary are broken down, making life more mysterious and precarious.

The rest of the chapter consists of a letter from Isabella to Ellen. Isabella says she regretted leaving Thrushcross Grange so suddenly, but that she can no longer go back. When she describes her return to Wuthering Heights, it's with a sense of helplessness. She had imagined that some member of the Heights household would be her ally against Heathcliff, but the others—Hareton, Hindley, and Joseph—are rough or crazy, and she's all alone. If only she had Hindley's pistol.

Isabella is a prisoner who isn't even allowed a cell. The description of her return is virtually a list of rooms she enters and is forced to leave. When Heathcliff first drops her off at the kitchen door, Hareton threatens to set his dog on her unless she quits the place. Then Hindley lets her back into the house through another door, and says she'll have to use Heathcliff's room. Hindley, in his madness, tries to force the lock on Heathcliff's room in order to shoot him, and Isabella is driven back into the kitchen. Joseph eventually shows her to a lumber room, which is even worse, and she ends up sleeping in a chair. When Heathcliff returns, Isabella reminds him that he still has the key to their room. Its not our room, he screams, it's mine, and mine alone. It's never made clear where she finally *does* sleep.

When Isabella throws her porridge to the floor, Joseph chides her, calling her "Miss Cathy." Isabella chafes under Heathcliff's tyranny, just as Cathy did under Hindley's, but Isabella has no friend to comfort her, as Cathy did.

NOTE: It's important that Isabella is the one who relates these events. Remember, you first learned of Hindley's cruelty through Cathy's diary. It's the victims with whom you identify, and Heathcliff here is no longer the tormented, but the tormentor.

CHAPTER 14

Edgar's refusal to communicate with Isabella seems cruel. He may have always seemed to lack passion, but does he lack warmth as well?

It's Ellen—the "bridge"—who goes over to Wuthering Heights, for the first time since Cathy's marriage. In her letter Isabella describes in detail the shambles the place has become. As an outsider, she can also see that Isabella, through neglect, looks a wreck. The only thing about the house that seems decent to her is Heathcliff.

The scene that follows offers you new definitions of love. At the same time it makes Heathcliff look sadistic.

When Heathcliff tells Ellen to arrange a meeting between him and Cathy or he will break into Thrushcross Grange, he draws distinctions between his love and Edgar's that remind you of the contrast in Cathy's feelings:

> If he loved with all the powers of his puny being, he couldn't love as much in eighty years as I could in a day. And Catherine has a heart as deep as I have; the sea could be as readily contained in that horse trough, as her whole affection monopolized by him.

This is one characterization of the difference between the stormy and calm types of love. Now add a third type, which is actually a mixture of the two: Isabella's infatuation with Heathcliff. Her willingness to put up with any brutality, such as watching him hang her dog, suggests that Isabella's love was as overwhelming and as all-forgiving as the love between Cathy and Heathcliff. Her love, however, was based on even less understanding than that between Cathy and Edgar. According to Heathcliff, Isabella saw him as a storybook hero.

In contrast to Heathcliff's avowal of love for Cathy is his unspeakably cruel treatment of Isabella. Not only does he speak to her abusively, but, as he tells

Ellen, he "experiments" with what she will endure. The fact that he can still feel shame for his behavior suggests that he has not yet sold his soul completely to the devil, but his shame doesn't make his behavior any more pardonable.

When Heathcliff sends Isabella off, he tells Ellen he has no pity. Then he goes on again about the differences between his love for Cathy, and Edgar's. What kind of demented love, you wonder, is this?

In Chapter 10 you were given one possible reason for Heathcliff's marriage to Isabella: he wants her property. Isabella gives you another reason: he wants to drive Edgar to some desperate act. Whatever his motivation, the loveless marriage seems to be Heathcliff's specialty. Later he will force one on Cathy's daughter and Linton. Is it possible that because of his own childhood he wants to prove that marriage (especially Edgar and Cathy's) has nothing to do with love (his own and Cathy's)?

CHAPTER 15

This chapter begins with a reminder of Cathy's deathlike state, and ends in a final gasp of passion for Heathcliff.

Heathcliff steals into her bedroom while Edgar is at church (unlike Isabella, Heathcliff always gets into places whether he's wanted or not), and embraces her. He's in despair because he realizes that Cathy is going to die. But this is no tender love scene. Cathy accuses him of thriving on her death, a death he caused. Her face shows a wild vindictiveness. When Heathcliff first lets go of her, his fingers leave blue marks in her skin.

Though Cathy softens a bit, Heathcliff does not. He accuses her of destroying them both when she married Edgar. When Cathy forgives him for leaving *her* for three years and begs to be forgiven, he refuses. "I forgive what you have done to me," he says. "I love *my* murderer—but *yours!* How can I?" This refusal may be one of the things that haunt him until his final "strange change" at the end of the book.

When they hear Edgar returning, Cathy clutches Heathcliff with mad resolution, declaring she'll die if he leaves. She faints, and Heathcliff puts the apparently lifeless body into Edgar's arms.

NOTE: In a more conventional novel there would have been a clearer death-bed resolution. Cathy would have declared a love for Heathcliff that her marriage to another could never dim or she would have said that she was, above all, Edgar's wife, and that there are greater things in life than love. But she does neither. Her unwillingness to leave Heathcliff may be her final statement, but she never tells him that she regrets marrying Edgar.

Note, too, that the scene isn't placed in the novel as if it were a climax. The story does not revert back to the present for reflection. There are two chapters to go before the story of the first generation ends. It will take the whole second half of the book to work out any kind of resolution.

Although the focus in this scene is on the lovers, Ellen is there, too. When Catherine first loses consciousness, the housekeeper thinks, "Far better that she should be dead, than lingering a burden and misery-maker to all about her." This is the cruelest comment she has made about anyone in the book. When you consider that Cathy is dying, you have to wonder how trustworthy any of her judgments of Cathy are.

CHAPTER 16

Two hours after Catherine becomes a mother, she dies.

In the last chapter Cathy said that she would find no peace in death, and yet she longs for the next "glorious" world and will pity those living on earth. Which is true? Ellen says that she likes to watch at a chamber of death because she sees a repose no earth or hell can break, but she's still sufficiently uncertain to interrupt her story and ask Lockwood, "Do you believe such people are happy in the other world, sir?"

Perhaps a character's opinion on whether Cathy has found peace tells you more about that character than about Cathy's fate. You see little of Edgar's grief. Although Ellen speaks only of his "exhausted anguish," it becomes clear later that Edgar believes Cathy is happy in heaven.

Heathcliff, on the other hand, is inconsolable. When Ellen says Cathy's life ended in a gentle dream, Heathcliff cries, "May she wake in torment!" and calls on her ghost to haunt him, as her murderer. He dashes his head against a tree trunk throughout the night, leaving blood on the bark. Despite the cruelty of his words, it's his anguish, not Edgar's, that you remember. His torment goes a long way toward blotting out his sins from your mind.

NOTE: Except for when they imagine a paradise for Mr. Earnshaw, Heathcliff and Cathy find no comfort in formal religion. As for the other characters,

Joseph's religious fervor is grotesque. Hindley uses religion for punishment rather than enlightenment, and Ellen's piety is too conventional to move you in any profound way.

Edgar follows the forms of religion, going to church every Sunday and getting strength from God. Yet it is Heathcliff and Cathy who speak in religious terms. When Heathcliff gets his first glimpse of Thrushcross Grange, for instance, he compares it to heaven. And Cathy considers herself in hell when she is separated from Heathcliff. The examples are endless, and explain why some readers call the love between Cathy and Heathcliff the strongest spiritual force in the novel.

Despite her sympathy for Edgar, Ellen lets Heathcliff in to view Cathy's body. He opens her locket to substitute his own lock of hair for Edgar's, trying to usurp the place next to her heart. But Ellen fittingly entwines the two tresses and encloses them together.

CHAPTER 17

On the morning after Cathy's funeral, Isabella bursts into Thrushcross Grange laughing, and her hysterical good humor persists, despite the fact that her light silk dress is streaming with snow and water; despite a deep, bloody cut under one ear; and despite her sincere sadness over Cathy's death. What has happened to her?

Certainly the first part of her story is no cause for joy. As she describes it to Ellen the night before, just after the funeral, Hindley tried without success to kill Heathcliff. Hindley locked the door in preparation, but Heathcliff managed to break in through the window and grab Hindley's pistol. In the struggle over the weapon, Hindley was wounded. Isabella's description of Heathcliff kicking and trampling Hindley, and knocking his head against the flagstones, is the most violent passage in the book. And this occurs at the point when you've regained your sympathies for Heathcliff.

NOTE: Just before he got out his pistol, Isabella told Hindley that treachery and violence are double-edged—"they wound those who resort to them, worse than their enemies." Certainly you have plenty of evidence of this so far. Characters who suffer try to find relief by passing the suffering on to others. Hindley behaves this way when his wife dies. Cathy is so hurt by the quarrel between Edgar and Heathcliff that she resolves to die in order to break both their hearts.

Isabella thrives on a dream of revenge, too, telling Ellen, "I'd rather [Heathcliff] suffer less, if I might cause his sufferings and he might know that I was the cause." Perhaps she cannot forgive him because she can never make him suffer as much as she has suffered.

She does her best, though, the morning after the funeral. She tells Heathcliff that Cathy would still be alive if it weren't for him; that Hindley's eyes—which Heathcliff tried to gouge out—are Catherine's; and that had Catherine become Mrs. Heathcliff, she would soon have become as disgusted with him as Isabella herself is.

Heathcliff throws a knife at her, which cuts her beneath her ear. While he's raving, she escapes. It's in this condition that she bursts into Thrushcross Grange.

The rest of the chapter closes the first half of the novel. Isabella flees to the south. Hindley dies in a drunken fit. Joseph says that before he left to fetch the doctor, Hindley was alone with Heathcliff, and far from death, which leaves you with an uneasy feeling. The characters have arranged themselves again according to their personalities at one of the two houses: Edgar, the baby Cathy, and Ellen are at Thrushcross Grange; Heathcliff, Hareton, and Joseph are at Wuthering Heights.

CHAPTER 18

Here begins the story of the second generation. Ellen Dean introduces the characters by comparing the young Cathy to her mother. This sense of continuity, of one generation bearing the sins of another, will continue through the rest of the novel. (There are 34 chapters; each generation gets 17.) Although one generation mirrors another, they are not exactly the same. Cathy, for instance is saucy and spoiled, but not to the extent her mother was, and the younger one adds a gentleness to a capacity for intense attachment.

In the last chapter Ellen told you that Edgar had become a recluse, perhaps the only possible reaction of a Thrushcross Grange character to the mad passions released in the preceding scenes. Edgar has also sheltered his daughter, who knows nothing of Heathcliff or of Wuthering Heights. But when Cathy is thirteen, Edgar learns that Isabella is dying. Thirteen is an age when you start to find things out about life. What Cathy finds out about is Wuthering Heights.

As she rides by, her dogs and Hareton's start to fight. History seems to be repeating itself, for it was because of a dog's attack that Lockwood was forced to spend the night at Wuthering Heights, and that the older Cathy was first brought to Thrushcross Grange. Dogs are associated with violence in the transition between the two worlds.

When Ellen finds Cathy, she and Hareton are enjoying themselves. But as soon as the subject of their parents' generation comes up, the youngsters quarrel. This is appropriate, since they will act out the problems that plagued their elders. Cathy, hearing that the owner of the house is not Hareton's father, mistakes Hareton for a servant. She's horrified to learn that this rough young man is her cousin. Again the Thrushcross Grange-Wuthering Heights conflict is being acted out: Cathy is civilized, educated, and socially proud; Hareton is foul mouthed, ignorant, and crude.

CHAPTER 19

In this chapter, Linton Heathcliff, the third member of the younger triangle, is introduced. His mother Isabella is dead, and Edgar has brought him home to Thrushcross Grange. The boy has an uncanny resemblence to Edgar, but his face has a sickly peevishness that his uncle's never had. Linton perks up only when Cathy feeds him tea out of a saucer, as though he were a baby. Edgar imagines that Cathy's company will stengthen the boy, but not a day passes before Joseph comes to take him to Heathcliff, his father. Little good can come of thrusting such a weakling into the harsh world of Wuthering Heights, and you begin to feel the inexorable power of its master.

CHAPTER 20

Linton is delivered to Heathcliff, who refers to the boy as his "property." He thinks of Linton less as a person than as an instrument for revenge. He says he'll treat Linton well so that he'll live to inherit Thrushcross Grange, and hire Edgar's and Hindley's descendants as laborers. So great is his obsession with revenge that he won't even let his regard for Hareton stand in his way.

NOTE: Notice how your attitude toward Heathcliff has changed. In the first half of the book he didn't get what he wanted (Cathy), so you felt sorry for him. Now he gets everything he wants, and it's difficult for you to feel anything but anger at him.

Ellen has to lie to get Linton out of Thrushcross Grange. It's wrong, but what else is there to do? The end of the chapter is even more chilling, as Linton cries, "Don't leave me! I'll not stay here! I'll not stay here!" Then the latch falls. . . .

CHAPTER 21

In this chapter Cathy meets Heathcliff for the first time. The Thrushcross Grange character (Edgar) can shelter his daughter from the Wuthering Heights side of life only so long, especially since Cathy is a curious child who loves to wander over the moors, much as her mother did.

The day that Heathcliff meets Cathy is her birthday, and the anniversary of her mother's death. But you don't see Heathcliff beating his head against a tree or throwing open a window to cry to his beloved. It is Edgar, you are told, who stays alone for hours by his dead wife's grave. The grief may be quiet, but it is heart-rending.

NOTE: Heathcliff outlines his scheme to Ellen— that Cathy and Linton will marry, thus consolidating Heathcliff's claim to the two estates. You know from the beginning of the book that he does in fact take possession of them, but he is not legally in the right, despite what he says.

Thrushcross Grange—a large house, with a park and tenants—is "entailed." This means that the possessor of the property has no control over who will inherit it; succession has already been worked out. In this case, the order of succession goes from the male son (Edgar), to the son of the male son (none), to the daughter (Isabella), to the son of the daughter (Linton). Linton won't be able to leave the place to his father. Heathcliff will claim it in his wife's name, but she never took possession, so Cathy, as Edgar's daughter, has a greater legal claim to the property.

Wuthering Heights is only a farmhouse, so inheritance is a simpler matter. Hindley may have mortgaged every inch of land he owned, and Heathcliff may be in possession as mortgagee, but Hareton, as Hindley's son, is heir to the title.

So Heathcliff will be a usurper until the day he dies.

The personalities of the younger generation become increasingly defined. When Heathcliff brings Cathy back to Wuthering Heights, you see that Linton has become selfish and ill-natured. The only time Linton shows any animation, according to Ellen, is when he mocks Hareton for not knowing how to read. Hareton may have enjoyed hanging puppies as a boy, but he doesn't seem so bad now. He may be rude and rough but he is sensitive, and he is more than willing to show Cathy around the property.

Cathy's reaction, when forbidden to write to Linton, is to slap Ellen—a reaction that should remind you of her mother. Remember how the elder Cathy resorted to pinching and slapping in Chapter 8? Yet whatever the similarities between the two, Cathy doesn't have her mother's grasp of character. She writes to Linton, and when she's found out, she announces that she's in love with him. In love? When the elder Cathy said she was in love with Edgar, she at least knew the boy. Her daughter's declaration of love reminds you more of Isabella's infatuation with Heathcliff.

CHAPTER 22

Edgar is sick, and so can't accompany Ellen and Cathy on their walk. Notice how little he participates in the action in the second half of the book. He comments on things, or forbids them, but he's never around when anything important happens.

It's appropriate that when Cathy wants something beyond her reach she ends up at Wuthering Heights or runs into Heathcliff. In order to reach some rose-hips, for example, she needs to climb over a wall near a locked door. Once she's on the other side, she can't get back over; neither she nor Ellen has the key. Just then Heathcliff comes along.

Heathcliff persuades Cathy that Linton is "dying" of love for her. This is a cruel satire on her mother's death. It's also untrue.

NOTE: If you think back over everything Heathcliff has said so far, you'll realize that he may have been hysterical, vengeful, or simply confused, but that he has never told such an elaborate, harmful lie. If you are like most readers, your estrangement from him is now complete.

CHAPTER 23

If Linton is dying, it can't be over love for Cathy. When she arrives, he says, "No—don't kiss me. It takes my breath—dear me!," and complains that writing all those letters wore him out. Still, they get along until the subject of the older generation comes up. This was true of Cathy and Hareton, too, when they first met. The problems of their elders seem to haunt these children, even without Heathcliff's help.

When Linton accuses Cathy's mother of hating her father and loving his, Cathy is so infuriated she pushes his chair over and he has a coughing fit. She is conciliatory, however (which Linton will never be). When Ellen and Cathy leave the room, they are recalled by a scream. Linton has slipped—on purpose?—to the hearthstone. He lies there writhing and crying.

CHAPTER 24

Cathy, against her father's orders, has been visiting Wuthering Heights. Most of this chapter is her story.

Showing once more how cruel she can be, Cathy makes fun of Hareton for priding himself on learning to read his name in the inscription over the door. In passing, you learn something new about Hareton. Before, he never quite understood why he was being mocked. Now he does catch on, even though it takes him a while. His pride, you learn, is quite different from Cathy's. Hers is an exercise in power, as she tries to put herself above him. His takes the form of a natural dignity, which has been affronted. If you think that Cathy's mother rejected Heathcliff because he was beneath her, then you will be able to see parallels in her daughter's behavior.

NOTE: Many readers find the story of the second generation a letdown after the high drama of the first, and certainly there is a sense of moderation here. Take the younger Cathy, for instance. Like her mother, she is given a fairly long speech comparing the stormy-calm sides of life through naturel imagery. The daughter's idea of happiness is rocking in a rustling green tree, with everything around her in motion. It's a wonderful speech, but it's more static than her mother's turbulent comparison of Edgar and Heathcliff, or her delirious longing for childhood.

Or think of Cathy's feeling for Linton. She finally shows some understanding of his character here, and he is given an endearing speech of his own. But Cathy's feeling seems closer to pity than to love. What a far cry from her mother's passion.

There are many other examples in the younger generation's behavior of a lessening of passion and a growth of moderation. This diminishment is built into the story.

In chapters 18 through 28 Heathcliff comes dangerously close to becoming a cardboard villain. His power is so inexorable that the younger generation can't stand up against him; they pale in comparison. Furthermore, a fight against total evil is rarely as interesting as a struggle among complex beings. What makes the fight between Hareton and Cathy so interesting is the fact that Heathcliff doesn't cause it.

The younger generation seldom use words such as *heaven* and *hell* or *angel* and *devil*. Ellen calls Cathy an "angel," but from her that's like saying "dear." Even Heathcliff avoids references to these unyielding forces. The absence of this mythic dimension makes you realize that compared to their parents, members of this generation have their feet on the ground.

The story of Cathy and Linton is told as it appears. Ellen rarely shifts from the past to the present. In addition, Cathy's story is the only one told by someone else. Think back on the first part of the book. You had Cathy's diary, Heathcliff's description of Thrushcross Grange, Cathy's delirium, Isabella's letter, Isabella's story. These accounts gave the impression that many mysterious things were happening at once. The story now has a more plodding rhythm.

Some readers think that this counterpoint between the first and second halves of the novel is an integral part of its theme. Others just want to get back to Cathy and Heathcliff.

CHAPTER 25

In the last chapter Edgar put a stop to Cathy's visits to Wuthering Heights. In this one he finally consents to her meeting Linton on the moors. Edgar is dying, and he hopes Linton will console her.

How you react to Edgar's wistful speech on death will depend on how you react to the Thrushcross Grange side of life. His tone is gentle. Compare the soft rhythms to the vigorous often abrupt, cadences in Heathcliff's speech. Edgar is magnanimous. He says he doesn't care whether Heathcliff gets what he wants, as long as Cathy is happy.

Yet there is also something lifeless in Edgar Linton. He seems to be as happy lying on his dead wife's grave as he is walking with his live daughter. And you may ask yourself why he can't check things out for himself once in a while. Why does he always rely on Ellen?

At the end of the chapter you learn that Linton Heathcliff is dying, too.

CHAPTER 26

A new element creeps into the book here: helpless terror. In his dream Lockwood was frightened by the ghost, but he was able to keep it from getting in. Edgar trembled when confronted with an angry Heathcliff, but that did not stop Edgar from striking him.

Linton can do nothing. When Cathy and Ellen meet him on the moors, he tries to appear well and cheerful, but his eyes wander fearfully toward Wuthering Heights. His terror has silenced even his complaints. Before he provoked, now he is only pitiable. (Note that it is only Linton, the most tedious character in the book, who shows this abject fear. Emily Brontë thinks highly of courage.)

As for Heathcliff, his behavior continues to get worse.

CHAPTER 27

The sense of doom is inescapable now. Edgar is closer to death. When Cathy and Ellen meet Linton on the moors he is even more fearful than before. Clues to the coming disaster come thick and fast. Linton cries that he has betrayed his old friend, so it's no surprise when Heathcliff shows up. Cathy may not be afraid to go to Wuthering Heights, but you are afraid for her. You've probably had dreams in which you feel this way; you know something awful is going to happen, even though you don't know what it is, and there's nothing you can do to stop it.

Once in Wuthering Heights, Heathcliff locks the door behind them, and his evil-scientist side reasserts itself: "Had I been born where laws are less strict, and tastes less dainty, I should treat myself to a slow vivisection of those two, as an evening's amusement." (Vivesection is surgery performed on live animals for experimental purposes.)

When Cathy grabs for the key, Heathcliff slaps her again and again on both sides of her face, and soon his plan is revealed: she will be his prisoner until morning, when he'll make her marry Linton. Heathcliff again mocks Edgar's type of love (remember the way he scorned it as he tormented Isabella). In the conversation that follows you get the most depressing versions of the two (Thrushcross Grange-Wuthering Heights) loves yet.

Cathy has often said that she loves her father more than she will ever love anybody. Is this all that Thrushcross Grange love comes down to? As much as you may love your parents, you must eventually love someone else—in a very different way—or forever remain a child.

As for the Wuthering Heights-type love, Heathcliff releases none of his former torrents of passion, but he makes one revealing statement about Cathy: "She's glad to be obliged to stay, I'm certain." Is this what love is, then, a form of imprisonment?

NOTE: You have seen at various points how Heathcliff is associated with imprisonment. As a youngster he was the one who was confined. From Cathy's diary you learn that he was thrown into the back kitchen. When he covered Edgar with applesauce, he was sent to a garret. Once locks and keys are actually mentioned, however, things change. After

Heathcliff returns transformed, he either keeps the keys (shutting Isabella out of the bedroom, for instance) or breaks the lock (as after his quarrel with Edgar).

During the second half of the book Heathcliff holds the keys. Remember the latch falling on Linton's cries. And now you have the worst case of all: Ellen is imprisoned for five nights and four days, with no word of Cathy's fate.

This change in Heathcliff's relationship to locks and keys reflects his growing mastery of the situation. As his power grows, your sympathy for him decreases. Emily Brontë makes you root for the underdog, whomever he may be.

CHAPTER 28

Ellen is released from her room. While sucking on candy, Linton tells how Cathy's mouth filled with blood when Heathcliff hit her. You've seen before how Emily Brontë juxtaposes the everyday with the horrifying or the mysterious. In this case the candy makes both Linton and his story all the more perverse. You have additional proof that cruelty has overshadowed love in Heathcliff's heart when Linton tells you how Heathcliff took Cathy's locket, which contained a picture of her father, and crushed it under his foot. How your feelings toward Heathcliff have changed since he replaced Edgar's hair with his own in Cathy's mother's locket!

Edgar wants to change his will so that Cathy's personal property will not automatically become her husband's (and thus Heathcliff's). Edgar wants to be certain that the property will be Cathy's for life, and then belong to her children. But the lawyer has become

Heathcliff's pawn, and arrives too late to alter the will.

Although Heathcliff turns away the servants Ellen sends to rescue Cathy, the girl frightens Linton into letting her out, and she is reunited with her father just before he dies. His death is peaceful, even blissful. He speaks of going to his wife and seeing his daughter later. Ellen and Cathy haven't told him, of course, about Heathcliff's latest trick. Edgar's happiness may depend on ignorance, but a peaceful ending seems only just for a man who led such a calm and caring life.

CHAPTER 29

NOTE: How many people has Heathcliff tormented? It's hard to keep track. Yet his cruelty doesn't bore you, since much of it—unlike what you see on television—is left to your imagination. Heathcliff only hinted, for instance, at what he was doing to Isabella. And when he describes his punishment of Linton for letting Cathy out, he will say only that:

> I brought him down one evening . . . and just set him in a chair, and never touched him afterwards. . . . In two hours I called Joseph to carry him up again; and since then my presence is as potent on his nerves as a ghost. . . .

What did Heathcliff do? Did he say anything? Did he just look at him? The description of a simple beating would have been less horrifying, for at least you would have known what happened.

In chapters 18 through 28 Heathcliff became almost the personification of evil. In this chapter he takes Cathy away from Thrushcross Grange to install her permanently at Wuthering Heights. In the next chapter he will watch Linton's death with complete indifference, perhaps even contributing to it. Yet now, to remind you that he is human, Emily Brontë throws in a scene so you recall Heathcliff's suffering. It begins when Cathy tells him with dreary triumph, *"Nobody loves you—nobody will cry for you when you die! I wouldn't be you!"* Knowing that his misery is greater than hers, she says, is her "revenge."

The truth of Heathcliff's suffering becomes more evident when he tells Ellen that he looked at Cathy's mother's dead face when Edgar's grave was dug, and that he has bribed the sexton to slide away the tops of her coffin and his own so that they will someday be united in death.

Heathcliff now gives his own version of events the night after Cathy's funeral when Hindley was beaten. The first time you heard the story, you feel Heathcliff acted with extreme cruelty and violence. In Heathcliff's version the Hindley incident is reduced to: "[T]hat accursed Earnshaw and my wife opposed my entrance. I remember stopping to kick the breath out of him. . . ." Which story should you believe? Should Heathcliff's behavior be excused because of his overwhelming grief? When Heathcliff dug open her grave and began to open her coffin, he felt her very presence. He hurried back to Wuthering Heights, talking to her, convinced he would see her upstairs in her room. Since then he has been searching for her constantly, but has never found her.

Heathcliff's story puts an entirely different light on the way he treated Hindley and Isabella that night. You can emphasize whatever aspect you wish: his torment over Cathy, or his indifference to his own violence. Certainly we have to sympathize to some extent with his tortured, sleepless nights since Cathy's death.

CHAPTER 30

This chapter consists largely of a story told to Ellen by Zillah, the current housekeeper at Wuthering Heights (and also the "lusty dame" of the first chapter). Ellen calls Zillah a "narrow-minded, selfish woman" for thinking that Cathy is proud and therefore refusing to wait on her. Certainly, Zillah comes off as hard hearted. She's indifferent to Cathy's suffering and to Linton's death. But just as Ellen's scolding tone makes her story more believable, so Zillah's disapproval of Cathy gives a realistic edge to the events surrounding Linton's death.

Zillah continues to accuse Cathy of pride when the girl rejects Hareton's attempts to make himself agreeable. The rejection is understandable, however, given his indifference to Cathy's lonely struggle at Linton's bedside. To some extent the quarrel between Cathy and Hareton has been forced on them by circumstances, although the roots of conflict were always there.

NOTE: Zillah ends her story with a summing up of Cathy's behavior: ". . . the more hurt she gets, the more venomous she grows." This seems to sum up the behavior of all the major characters except Edgar. Isabella, Cathy, and Cathy's mother all speak of revenge as a way of dealing with their suffering. Against this backdrop you may not find Heathcliff quite so evil. And yet his type of vengeance is of a different, more sinister quality. Like Hindley, he takes out his suffering on the innocent, even on children. As he explains in Chapter 11, "the tyrant grinds down his slaves and they don't turn against him; they crush those beneath them."

Until now you've seen people hurting others, and being hurt in return. The only way characters have broken out of this vicious circle has been to break off the relationship—through flight (as in Isabella's case) or to have it end through death. In the last few chapters Hareton and Cathy will manage to create a new pattern. Heathcliff may, too.

CHAPTER 31

Ellen's story ended with the last chapter. Now you are back in the present, with Lockwood, who visits Wuthering Heights once more to say he's leaving, and to take another look at the lovely young widow. He has expressed an interest in her before, at the end of Chapter 14 (". . . let me beware of the fascination that lurks in Catherine Heathcliff's brilliant eyes"), and at the beginning of Chapter 25, when Ellen suggested that he marry Cathy. Nothing comes of this, however, and he dismisses her now with great arrogance. "Living among clowns and misanthropists," he had reasoned, "she probably can't appreciate a better class of people, when she meets them." But it is true that Cathy is as unpleasant as she was the first time they met. Lockwood now defends Hareton, playing the role of peacemaker instead of lover. But the question has been raised: Is it possible that Cathy will consider remarrying.

In your one glimpse of Heathcliff you see the first crack in his plan of revenge. "It will be odd, if I thwart myself!" he says.

CHAPTER 32

About a year later Lockwood passes through Yorkshire and decides to stop at Thrushcross Grange. He is told that Ellen has gone to Wuthering Heights, so he heads over there. The change in Wuthering Heights is astonishing. The gate is unlocked, the fragrance of flowers permeates the air, and a scene of young love is played out at an open window. A sweet-voiced girl is teaching a handsome, respectably dressed lad how to read. She kisses him, and slaps him playfully. The two, of course, are Cathy and Hareton. Emily Brontë withholds their identities at first to emphasize their complete transformation.

The scene is a union of the best of both houses. Books once belonged only at Thrushcross Grange. For the older Cathy and Heathcliff they were objects of repression; as children, they threw religious books into the fire in an act of rebellion. For Edgar reading was a way to escape from problems; he shut himself up with his books when Cathy fell into a fit. Suddenly, books have become a medium through which love can flow. At the same time, physical love—the Wuthering Heights side of love—is also allowed to find expression. Lockwood slinks around back, thinking about what he has missed. Ellen Dean, who is happy now, fills you in on what has happened in the past year.

When she returns to Wuthering Heights, Ellen finds Cathy and Hareton still fighting. Cathy soon begins to make overtures of friendship, however, as Hareton did before. It is a slow process, but finally they come to grips with their feelings and confess to the pain they have been causing each other. Each puts the emphasis on his own suffering rather than on the wrongdoing of the other. (Compare this to the wild accusations the older Cathy and Heathcliff hurl at each other on her deathbed.) Once Hareton accepts Cathy's present of a book, the vicious cycle of suffering has been broken. They have forgiven each other.

CHAPTER 33

Cathy brings Thrushcross Grange—in the form of flowers from her old house—to Wuthering Heights. To do so she has Hareton uproot Joseph's beloved black currant trees. Later she sticks primroses in her new friend's porridge. You may find this silly, but it's undeniable that the household is changing.

Even Heathcliff begins to change. When he grabs Cathy as if to tear her to pieces, his fingers suddenly relax as he glares intently into her face and sees her mother's eyes. Heathcliff sees his beloved everywhere, in the flagstones, in the clouds, in the trees. In Hareton he sees his lost youth. These images paralyze this once violent and domineering man. Now that everything is in place, he says, he can't lift a finger to carry out his revenge. Why can't he act? Why does revenge no longer give him pleasure? Ellen suggests that his conscience has made his life into an earthly hell, but Heathcliff shows no more signs of a guilty conscience now than before. Maybe there's an explanation of Heathcliff's behavior in the final chapter.

CHAPTER 34

You read just four chapters ago that Heathcliff had complete control of Wuthering Heights and Thrushcross Grange. Now he doesn't have control even over himself. He can't eat or sleep. The reasons for both this final illness—this "strange change"—and for his death are ambiguous. Depending on how you feel about Heathcliff, you can emphasize either of two interpretations: he has finally been consumed by his own infernal passion, or he has been united spiritually with Catherine. Either way the love between young Hareton and Cathy intensifies his sense of loss and is inextricably linked with his change.

You can support the idea of an infernal passion: his is a strange joy, accompanied by shivering, and bloodshot eyes; he focuses on things that aren't there, things that bring him both rapture and anguish. His appearance is so strange that one night Ellen is convinced he's a goblin, a ghoul, or a vampire. How do we know where he came from? she asks. Even when her common sense is restored in the morning, she is frightened of him, and won't sit with him. He seems to commune with Cathy's ghost, with wild endearment and with suffering. When speaking of making a will, he wishes he could destroy all his property so no one would get it. He says he has done no injustice to anybody. He rejects making peace with God, and instead insists on the mingling of the coffins. He dies with a sneer on his face.

Or you can support the idea of spiritual union with Catherine: Heathcliff says he has been on the threshold of hell, and now is in sight of heaven (which he has always equated with Cathy). Hareton and young Cathy, who should understand his love better than Ellen, particularly since they have just found their own, emphasize Heathcliff's happiness in their descriptions of him. Heathcliff doesn't bother the young lovers now. In fact, he encourages Hareton, whom he sees as a younger version of himself. He begins to view Hareton as a person instead of an instrument of revenge. After he brings up the subject of the will and the lawyer, he dismisses it. Questions of inheritance, which once obsessed him, mean nothing to him now. He has been trying unsuccessfully to see Cathy's ghost for years. Perhaps he sees it now because, in relinquishing his revenge, he has also forgiven her. Finding peace in Cathy's love seems to offer him greater spiritual satisfaction than any conventional religion. His face is exhultant in death. Perhaps the sneer is only Ellen's fancy.

Do the ghosts of Heathcliff and Catherine still live and walk about? Perhaps, if you think theirs was an infernal passion. But the final sentence of the book is one of peace. Musing beside their graves, Lockwood wonders how "anyone could ever imagine unquiet slumbers for the sleepers in that quiet earth."

A STEP BEYOND

Tests and Answers

TESTS

Test 1

1. After his first visit to Wuthering Heights, Mr. _____
   Lockwood plans to return because he
   A. has been so graciously received by the
      host
   B. sees in Heathcliff a kindred spirit
   C. is curious to learn the secret of Heathcliff's
      dark despair

2. Heathcliff responds to the account of Mr. _____
   Lockwood's dream by
   A. forbidding him to sleep in the same room
      again
   B. ridiculing the dream as the hallucinations
      of an overactive imagination
   C. crying out for Catherine at the broken
      window

3. Heathcliff _____
   A. has been so named after Mr. Earnshaw's
      son who had died at birth
   B. tries to ingratiate himself with the
      Earnshaw children when he is first
      brought to Wuthering Heights
   C. uses Ellen to cause trouble between
      Catherine and Hindley

4. The night Hindley orders the house barred to _____
   Catherine and Heathcliff, Heathcliff returns
   very late to report that

    A. he and Cathy plan to be married

    B. Cathy has been lost on the moors

    C. Cathy's ankle has been injured and she is staying at the Linton home

5. Hindley's mistreatment of Heathcliff began with his _____

    A. despair and drunkenness after the death of his wife Frances

    B. jealousy of the orphan boy when he first came to the Earnshaw home

    C. realization of the dark, brooding evil in Heathcliff's character

6. Which statement is true? _____

    A. Heathcliff is informed by Nelly that Catherine has agreed to marry Edgar

    B. Heathcliff catches Hareton when the child is dropped from the stairs by the drunken Hindley

    C. Heathcliff begs Catherine to run off and marry him instead of Edgar

7. When Heathcliff returns after an absence of three years _____

    A. he tries to win back Catherine with his newly acquired riches

    B. he reveals that he is really descended from nobility

    C. Isabella falls in love with him

8. Which statement is *not* true? _____

    A. Both Catherine and Heathcliff at different points in the novel subject themselves to a long period of fasting

    B. Catherine, in her delirium, pleads for death to free her of her loveless marriage

C. Edgar, in the belief that Catherine is faking her illness, keeps himself aloof during her "convalescence"

9. The final meeting of Catherine and Heathcliff _____ is filled
   A. only with passionate embracing and professions of eternal love
   B. with despair, anguish, recriminations, and passion
   C. with anger at the cruelty of fate that has deprived the lovers of happiness

10. On the last night of Catherine's life, she _____
    A. gives birth to a daughter
    B. predicts that Heathcliff will soon follow her to the grave
    C. extracts a promise from Heathcliff and Edgar to end their quarrel

11. Is *Wuthering Heights* a novel about love? Discuss.

12. One of the few characters who doesn't get to tell part of this story is Edgar. What is the effect of this?

13. Compare Wuthering Heights and Thrushcross Grange.

14. Is Emily Brontë a mystic or a social realist?

15. Is Heathcliff the hero of the book? Discuss.

Test 2

1. By the end of the first half of the novel which _____ of the following characters have died?
   A. Hareton and Catherine
   B. Catherine and Hindley
   C. Hindley and Isabella

2. Which statement is *not* true of Heathcliff?   _____
    A. He intends to take possession of both
       Wuthering Heights and Thrushcross
       Grange through his son
    B. He refuses to accept the responsibility of
       raising his son after his wife dies
    C. He feels the same degree of affection for
       Hindley's son as for his own son

3. Cathy's love letters to Wuthering Heights are   _____
    addressed to
    A. Hareton
    B. Linton
    C. both cousins

4. Heathcliff's scheme for revenge is   _____
    A. thwarted by Linton's death
    B. advanced by Linton's death
    C. the most powerful expression of his
       nature

5. To accomplish his goal Heathcliff   _____
    A. imprisons Cathy in his house
    B. forces Linton to marry Cathy
    C. both A and B

6. The lawyer arrives   _____
    A. just in time for Edgar to change his will
       before he dies
    B. too late to change Edgar's will because he
       was involved in rescuing Cathy from
       Wuthering Heights
    C. too late to change Edgar's will because he
       had been bought off by Heathcliff

7. When Lockwood returns to Wuthering _____
   Heights after a long absence, he finds the gate
   to the house is open, a sign that
   A. Hareton is as careless as the previous
      master
   B. Wuthering Heights has been abandoned
   C. Heathcliff is dead

8. Cathy is saved from Heathcliff's fury when _____
   A. Hareton protects her from further blows
   B. Heathcliff loses his desire for revenge
   C. Ellen Dean intervenes and threatens to call
      the constable

9. In the few days before his death, Heathcliff _____
   A. arranges with the sexton to open his and
      Catherine's coffins on one side so their
      bones will mingle
   B. finally accepts Cathy and Hareton as his
      heirs
   C. radiates a strange happiness

10. You hear most of the narrative of *Wuthering* _____
    Heights from
    A. Mr. Lockwood
    B. Ellen Dean
    C. Zillah

11. How does Emily Brontë's use of narrators affect the
    novel?

12. Discuss the presentation of revenge.

13. Compare the two generations.

14. Discuss Brontë's style.

15. In what way is *Wuthering Heights* a novel of child-
    hood?

ANSWERS

Test 1

1. B **2.** C **3.** A **4.** C **5.** B **6.** B

7. C **8.** C **9.** B **10.** A

11. If you do not think this is a novel about love, begin by stating what it *is* about—revenge, rebellion, or whatever. Discuss how this is different from love. Refer to specific relationships, scenes, and plot lines in the book to show why the theme you've chosen is more important than the theme of love.

If you do think this is a novel about love, begin by describing what kind of love Brontë is presenting. Then choose specific characters, relationships, and scenes that illustrate this type of love. Show how the book as a whole develops the theme of love, by comparing and contrasting different loves in the book (Heathcliff's and Edgar's, for example, or the two Cathys') and discussing the ending as a resolution of the theme of love.

12. First briefly discuss the book's complicated narrative structure—who gets to tell which parts of the story, and how these different narratives affect your point of view. Then focus on Edgar. Discuss his personality and his role in the book. What kind of story might he have told? How would that have changed the novel's point of view or its themes?

13. In discussing the two houses you should look at all the elements of the book, since the houses are the two poles around which the novel is structured. Begin by defining the qualities associated with each house, then show how these qualities are developed. Contrast the physical aspects of the places themselves as settings. Compare two characters, such as Heathcliff and Edgar, as the prime examples of the two worlds, and then discuss other characters as you see fit. The question does not ask you to judge which house is better or which one Brontë prefers, but you could discuss that, too. Or, if you don't think one is better, discuss the effect of the perpetual tension between the two.

14. You should discuss both possibilities briefly in your opening paragraph—which elements of this novel seem mystical and which seem realistic? Then choose one side or the other to explore at length. You may also argue that she is both, but if you do so you should explain how such seemingly opposite outlooks work together in her writing. Be sure to support your argument with specific evidence from the novel. For example, talk about her mystical belief in spirits when Cathy's ghost speaks to Heathcliff, or her realistic discussion of inheritance and property rights.

15. Begin by defining *hero*. You can define it either as the main character or as the most sympathetic character in the book. If you're judging him as the main character, show whether he is central to the plot and to the novel's themes. If you don't think he is the main character, argue who you think is more important.

If you're judging Heathcliff as a sympathetic character, begin by discussing his personality and what happens to him. Show how he fits into the novel's moral outlook, and what his dramatic appeal is. If you don't think he is the most sympathetic character, discuss the character you find most sympathetic, and compare that character to Heathcliff.

Test 2
1. B   2. C   3. B   4. C   5. C   6. C
7. C   8. B   9. C   10. B

11. Begin by analyzing the novel's narrative structure. Give examples of the different narrators. Then discuss the effect Brontë creates by switching narrators. Here are some possibilities: suspense is built; extraordinary events seem believable; different points of view are given equal weight and you must decide which interpretation is most valid. Refer to specific episodes, and try to examine the effect of each narrator's tone.

12. Begin by discussing how revenge operates in the novel. Look at Heathcliff's desire for revenge: Is it just? Does it go too far? Be sure to discuss specific episodes, and show both how Heathcliff feels and how Emily Brontë seems to feel about his revenge. Go on to discuss other characters: Hindley, Cathy Earnshaw, Isabella, Edgar, Hareton—both those who do and those who do not seek revenge.

Relate the theme of revenge to the other themes on the novel: forgiveness, suffering, love, and continuity between generations. Do you think revenge is the major theme? Why or why not? How does Emily Brontë seem to regard revenge?

13. Begin by presenting the two halves of the novel, each half devoted to one generation. Discuss how the characters and the plot of one generation are repeated in the next. Then focus on some of these mirrored pairs, such as the two Cathys, or a pair of events, such as the two marriages. In each pair discuss both the similarities and differences. In your concluding paragraph sum up how the two generations are alike and how they are different, and discuss what Brontë may be trying to express through this contrast.

14. Analyze different aspects of Brontë's style (discuss specific passages). Relate her style to the style of her times and discuss her use of local dialect. Be sure to point out 1. the natural imagery; 2. the supernatural imagery; and 3. the violence of her language. How do these stylistic elements add to the tone and mood of the novel? Relate them also to the novel's themes: How does this type of language express Brontë's moral outlook?

15. This is an open-ended question. You may discuss various aspects of the book that seem eternally youthful: Why does its themes appeal to young readers, for instance?

Why does the novel seem as though a young author wrote it? Be sure to refer to the events, themes, and characters of the book. For example, you can discuss Heathcliff and Cathy as characters who in a sense never grow up. Or you can discuss Emily Brontë's love of childhood and its associated freedoms. (What happens to people when they grow up in the novel?) Or you can examine how the personalities of the characters are determined by their youthful experiences (compare Heathcliff and Cathy Earnshaw, or Cathy Linton and Linton Heathcliff). You could also discuss the way children are treated, and how that relates to the themes. Or discuss how the resolution of the novel is worked out by a younger generation (Hareton and Cathy). Whatever you choose to discuss, cover enough of the novel to show that you know the book well, and that the theme of childhood is truly a major element of the novel.

Term Paper Ideas

1. Compare two of the characters, such as Heathcliff and Edgar, the two Cathys, Heathcliff and Hareton, Ellen Dean and Heathcliff or Ellen Dean and Cathy, or Hareton and Linton.

2. Show why Heathcliff's role in the novel could have been played by a supernatural creature such as the devil.

3. Show how sympathy is created for Heathcliff despite his evil deeds.

4. Show why Heathcliff's fight is directed against the oppressive landed classes.

5. Explore the nature of Heathcliff's "strange change."

6. Explain why Cathy marries Edgar.

7. Discuss the different types of love—that between Heathcliff and Cathy and that between Hareton and Cathy. Why do you prefer one over the other?

8. Discuss Joseph as a comic character.

9. Explore the characteristics of Ellen Dean as a reliable narrator.

10. Discuss who you think is the dominant character in the book.

11. Describe what makes the characters in *Wuthering Heights* different from those in other books.

12. Decide with whom Brontë wants you to identify at various points in the novel. What light does this identification shed on the characters and themes?

13. Analyze the psychological progression of Chapter 3.

14. Analyze Cathy's mad scene in Chapter 8. In what ways is her delirium a "higher" truth?

15. Analyze the fight between Heathcliff and Cathy on her deathbed. Who's right?

16. Compare Isabella's version of the night after Cathy's funeral (in Chapter 17) to Heathcliff's (in Chapter 29).

17. Discuss the role of locks and keys in the novel.

18. Describe how the author portrays books in the novel.

19. Discuss the role of windows in *Wuthering Heights*.

20. Analyze the portrayal of the supernatural in the novel.

21. Some readers think there is a tension between the rigid structure of the book and the wildness of the language. Explore that tension and give examples.

22. Discuss what you think is the climax of the novel.

Further Reading

CRITICAL WORKS

Cecil, David. *Early Victorian Novelists*. New York: Bobbs-Merrill, 1935, pp. 157–203. The first exploration of the stormy-calm, Wuthering Heights-Thrushcross Grange contrast.

Fike, Francis. "Bitter Herbs and Wholesome Medicines," *Nineteenth Century Fiction*, 23 (1968). A religious reading.

Gregor, Ian, ed. *Twentieth Century Interpretations of the Brontës*. Englewood Cliffs, N.J.: Prentice-Hall, 1970. Six of the essays are on *Wuthering Heights*. C. P. Sanger's broke ground on the structural complexity of the book.

Hanson, Lawrence and E. M. *The Four Brontës*. London: Oxford University Press, 1949. Biographical.

Hinkley, Laura L. *Charlotte and Emily*. New York: Hastings House, 1945. Biographical.

Kettle, Arnold. "Wuthering Heights," in *An Introduction to the English Novel*. London: Hutchinson, 1951, pp. 139–55. Heathcliff as a morally superior rebel.

Moser, Thomas. "Conflicting Impulses in *Wuthering Heights*." *Nineteenth Century Fiction*, 17 (1962). The Freudian interpretation.

Schorer, Mark. "Fiction and the Analogical Matrix," in *The World We Imagine*. New York: Farrar Straus, 1948, pp. 28–34. Points out the natural imagery and the violence in the language.

Van Ghent, Dorothy. "On *Wuthering Heights*," in *The English Novel: Form and Function*. New York: Rhinehart, 1953, pp. 153–71. Explores the doubled structure of the book, and substitutes dissolution-containment theme for the stormy-calm contrast.

RELATED WORKS

Brontë, Charlotte. *Jane Eyre*.

Hatfield, C. W. *The Complete Poems of Emily Jane Brontë*. New York: Columbia University Press, 1941.

Glossary

Joseph's speech may give you some problems at first, since he uses dialect a lot, and since the words are written phonetically to give you an idea of his accent. Read a few sentences out loud, and you'll catch on. Words with a long *e* are usually given a long *a* instead. Hence, *clane* for "clean," and *stale* for "steal." "Ow" is usually *ah;* "down" becomes *dahn;* "how," *hah;* "doubt," *daht.* A long *i* often becomes a long *e.* "Night" and "sight" are *neeght* and *seeght.* "Die" is *dee.*

Here are some words you'll get used to quickly.

Aw I
'Baht Without
Bud But
Frough From
Hor Her
I' In
Mun Must
Nobbut No one else
Norther Neither
Nowt Nothing, a worthless person
Shoo She
Sud Should
'T It
T' The
Tuh To
Un One
Un' And
War Worse

Other unusual words in *Wuthering Heights* are the following:
Bairnies Bairns, children.

Basilisk Spell-binding, fatal; a basilisk is a legendary reptile with fatal breath and glance.

Beck Small stream.

Boards Shutters or doors.

Brach Bitch hound.

Cant 1. Talk with affected piety; 2. Lively, vigorous, cheerful.

Chuck Chicken.

Clothes press Clothes cupboard.

Cockatrice Legendary serpent with a deadly glance, hatched by a reptile from a cock's egg on a dung hill.

Comminations Denunciations.

Crahnr Coroner (assimilated to crown).

Deaved Broken with violence.

Den Narrow valley or ravine.

Dunnock Hedge sparrow.

Een Eyes.

Eft Pewt.

Fain 1. Willingly; 2. rather.

Faishion Have the cheek to.

Flaysome Frightening.

Flighted Scared.

Frame Go.

Gait Manner.

Galloway Small horse or pony.

Gans Goes.

Gaumless Without understanding.

Girn Snarl.

Girt Great.

Grat Cried, wept.

Happen Perhaps.

Harried Dragged.

Hob Projection at the back or side of a fireplace where something can be kept warm.

Jocks Jugs.

Kirk   Church.

Laced   Beat, whipped.

Laith   Barn.

Leveret   A hare in its first year.

Lig   Lie.

Ling   Heather.

Linnets   Finches.

Lugs   Ears.

Madling   A mad person, a simpleton.

Marred   Peevish.

Meansful   Becoming, proper, seemly, decent.

Meeterly   Moderately.

Mells on   Meddles with, occupies with.

Milo   Greek athlete who was eaten by wolves after getting trapped in the tree he was trying to tear apart.

Mim   Prim, affectedly modest.

Mither   Mother.

Mools   Earth.

Nab   Projecting part of a hill or rock.

Nave   Fist.

Offald   Worthless.

Ousels   Blackbirds or thrushes.

'Owd Nick   Old Nick, the devil.

Piked   Picked.

Pining   Torturing, receiving pain.

Plisky   Trick.

Scroop   Back of the cover of a book.

Scuttle   Metal pail for carrying coal.

Settle   Wooden bench with arms, a high solid back, and an enclosed foundation that can be a chest.

Side out   Move away, clear out.

Sizar   Scholarship student.

'Sizes   Assizes, superior court in English counties for trial of civil and criminal cases.

Skift   Move away quickly, change places.

Sough Small bog.
Starved Suffered from the cold.
Tent Care.
Thible Stick or spatula used for stirring.
Thrang Busy.
Throstles Song thrushes.

The Critics

Heathcliff betrays one solitary human feeling, and that is *not* his love for Catherine; which is a sentiment fierce and inhuman: a passion such as might boil and glow in the bad essence of some evil genius; a fire that might form the tormented centre—the ever-suffering soul of a magnate of the infernal world: and by its quenchless and ceaseless ravage effect the execution of the decree which dooms him to carry Hell with him wherever he wanders. No; the single link that connects Heathcliff with humanity is his rudely confessed regard for Hareton Earnshaw—the young man whom he has ruined; and then his half-implied esteem for Nelly Dean.

> —*Charlotte Brontë, preface to the 1850 edition of* Wuthering Heights

Heathcliff and Cathy die without making a fact of the oneness they both feel is theirs. To Emily Brontë, their marriage is unthinkable. It can happen only as distant parody: the marriage of Hareton and Cathy the younger at the end of the book. Hareton is a watered-down Heathcliff; Cathy is a pale, though still vivacious, replica of her mother. [*Wuthering Heights* and *Jane Eyre*] end similarly: a relatively mild and ordinary marriage is made after the spirit of the masculine universe is controlled or extinguished.

> —*Richard Chase, in* Twentieth Century Interpretations, *1947*

Heathcliff's revenge may involve a pathological condition of hatred, but it is not at bottom merely neurotic. It has a moral force. For what Heathcliff does is to use against his enemies with complete ruthlessness their own weapons, to turn on them (stripped of their romantic veils) their own standards, to beat them at their own game. The weapons he uses against the Earnshaws and Lintons are their own weapons of money and arranged marriages. He gets power over

them by the classic methods of the ruling class, expro-
priation and property deals.
> —*Arnold Kettle*, An Introduction to
> the English Novel, 1951

Any choice between "the Heights" and "the
Grange," any writing up and writing down, will be the
manufacture of the critic, not the novelist. Emily Brontë's places of the heart are not stages in the develop-
ment of the highest self, but totally different ideas of
love, speaking different languages. What we do in
reading the book is learn to understand the two archi-
tectures, and begin to measure the full and complex
implications of their opposition, revealed to us with
scrupulous objectivity.
> —*Mark Kinkead-Weekes, in* Twentieth
> Century Interpretations, 1970

None of the other Victorians can successfully
describe a death scene. Awestruck at so tremendous a
task, they lose their creative nerve; their imaginations
boggle and fail, and they fill up the gaps left by its
absence with conventional formulas. A stagey light of
false tragic emotion floods the scene; the figures
become puppets, squeaking out appropriately touch-
ing or noble sentiments. But Emily Brontë's eagle imagination gazed with as undaunted an eye on death, as
on everything else. The light she sheds on it is the same
light that pervades her whole scene, and it is the light of
day.
> —*David Cecil*, Early Victorian
> Novelists, 1935